I0474862

THE THEORY OF CULTURE

A fundamental leadership tool to build sustainable and spontaneous organizations

Ashish Marathe

The Theory of Culture

Dedicated to my team-mates at the organization I first belong to –

Aai and Baba, my parents,
Supriya, my wife,
Vihaan, our 5 year old son,

And

The 'culture' at our home, the ever-present, non-visible member of the team.

Contents

Preface

Culture is a leader's primary responsibility. It is also the primary tool at his/her disposal to strengthen the organization. This book speaks of what culture in an organization means and how amazingly it can work to build a strong organization. It is meant for every person in a leadership role at any level in an organization. It is also meant for every person who wants to become a leader. I am not sure when, but I have developed a strong fascination for the concept of organizational culture.

I am born and brought up in Goa, India. I qualified as a chartered accountant in year 2003. Until then, my sole focus was on absorbing the technical knowledge of the field of accountancy and finance, and developing the acumen to deal with the intricacies of applying that knowledge. I took up my first job in 2003, and from then to now, I have worked for more than fifteen years in different capacities across five organizations. Somewhere during this journey, I started thinking of culture, or pieces of it. I had the benefit of working in organizations of various types and sizes. A couple of them are in niche businesses with less than twenty five employees each. A couple of them are huge organizations with more than hundred thousand people each, spread across the globe. The fifth organization is a mid-sized manufacturing group with five hundred people. I also spent time with different kinds of people, each with a different perspective and a different driver. I interacted with people from several parts of India, and the globe. I stayed for three months in Zurich, which gave me a taste of a different culture from close quarters. Each of the people I interacted with and each of the organization I worked for enriched my knowledge of culture immensely. I became a keen student of the concept of organizational culture and how it affects performance. The various cultures I experienced taught me a lot – some taught me 'how to do' things, many others 'how not to'.

One of my bosses always spoke of himself and only himself. Most of his sentences would start with the word 'I'. Another boss was very particular about the accuracy of English in my reports. He would insist on two or three proof readings before the report was finalized. I had a peer who was one of the most brilliant guys I ever met, but his lack of people skills ensured that he never delivered to his potential. I had a subordinate who once had a long and strong argument with me because I had asked him to deviate from a process that I myself had installed and trained him on.

I started analyzing every experience of mine with the curiosity of a child, and this helped me develop my own thought process towards the concept of culture. I got opportunities to use these concepts at my job place and to convince leadership on their importance. I learnt that culture building is usually not a priority area for an organization, especially the small and medium organizations. But I also learnt that culture is the strongest force in an organization, and if an effort is put into improving culture, the life of the organization can become much easier. Culture is the most fundamental tool a leader can employ to build 'sustainable' and 'spontaneous' organizations.

There is no single guide that explains what exactly culture is, and how it can be worked on for the benefit of the organization. I experienced a strong urge within me to express all that I had experienced and reflected on with a view to creating a 'textbook' of culture, in a simple and user-friendly form. That is how the idea of this book emerged. To be frank, there is no rocket science that I have presented in this book. I have only written on the most simple and fundamental culture concepts. Sometimes, concepts are not given their due importance because they are simple. This book attempts at correcting this situation by explaining what simple things can do and putting all the simple things at one place for ease of reference.

While the idea of this book got generated over several months, once I started to write, it was as if I was on 'autopilot' mode. The form that the book adopted, the structure of chapters, or the choice of examples cited - all came through from an unknown source. My sub-conscious took over the charge, and 'I' came in only at the end of the project, to do checks on spelling, grammar, consistency, and other aesthetics. It was truly a divine experience.

I hope you will enjoy reading this book. But more importantly, I hope this book enriches you with knowledge on importance of culture in an organization, and what it takes to build the right culture.

A 'cultural' change that has taken place in the field of books is that books have become 'interactive'. A book is no longer one-way traffic and it should not be as well. The power of 'we' is much stronger than that of 'I'. Your feedback will be very important for me. Please do write to me if you like this book, or if you do not like it. Please tell me if you agree with a concept, or if you reject it. Any emotion that you experience towards the matter in this book, any different perspective that you bring in – please share with me. Writing this book has been a great learning experience. Your participation in this process will allow me to keep learning.

This book is set in an ancient era, and deals with administration of a kingdom as a model for culture building. The administration of ancient kingdoms, as far as I am aware, was largely done by men. Hence, wherever I have made a general reference to a team member of the administration team, I have used the words 'he' or 'his'. This of course, is not intended to indicate any gender bias. Our 'culture' today in this regard is much different from what it was centuries back, with equal or more participation from women in some parts of the globe, and increasing women participation in the rest, in every field in which they had limited access earlier.

I take this opportunity to thank the organizations I worked for, and the wonderful people I interacted with during this period. They are the real source of the material that has taken the shape of this book.

Ashish Marathe

ashish.m.marathe@gmail.com

Section I

The Problem

A Friend

Arrives

I t was early morning. The dock area on the coast had its usual attendance. A few bullock carts were parked on the side with their drivers spending time chatting with one another. They were waiting for the fishermen to arrive with their catch of the day. Once the fishermen would reach, the slow life until then would suddenly catch pace. The staff on the fishing boats and the bullock cart drivers would then get busy sorting the fish, deciding on pricing, and loading them on the carts. The carts would then move to the local market nearby so that the fish could be sold to the customers. This was a daily routine. They were all residents of the coastal city called 'Praami'. Praami was the capital city of the 'Paryaakul' kingdom, a large kingdom with King 'Viklav' as its ruler. Paryaakul was a kingdom blessed with nature's gifts in abundance, and a variety of them. It had a long belt of sea on the West side, a similar belt of mountains in the centre, and plains in the east. A large number of rivers emanated from the mountains and flew westwards. King Viklav was the twenty first King from his family since the time the first King had won the territory from the earlier dynasty. King Viklav's family was always known to be a dynasty that cared for its people and Paryaakul was known to be a happy state across the entire continent. However, over last three generations, the kingdom was slowly losing its glory.

While the dock area was witnessing the usual activity, there were some unusual visitors too. There was King Viklav himself standing at some distance away along with a few of his soldiers and assistants. Giving him company was his Minister for Foreign Affairs 'Paadvik'. Both King Viklav and Paadvik were sitting in the royal chariot. They were waiting for a royal guest by the name 'Mitr Prabuddh'. They had intentionally chosen a place hidden behind a large family of mangroves, since they did not want to disturb the normal activity at the dock, or to draw any extra attention in advance. Mitr Prabuddh was a spiritual scholar. It was Paadvik who had first heard of Prabuddh, when on a tour of a distant kingdom. Prabuddh, though a spiritual scholar, liked the title 'Mitr' meaning friend to be associated with him, rather than 'Guru'. Paadvik had heard a lot of praise about Prabuddh from the head of the University he had visited. Prabuddh had apparently helped improve the quality of the University through very simple and practical actions, helping the University to be known as the best in the continent over a span of three years. Prabuddh, as told to Paadvik, had spent years on gaining knowledge of and practicing spirituality, but had great interest in the management of organizations and how the quality of management could be improved. Paadvik had a custom of reporting all important observations to Viklav after the completion of any tour. Accordingly, on returning from his journey covering the visit to the University, he had reported to Viklav what he had heard about Prabuddh. Viklav got very interested to know more

8

about Prabuddh. Viklav was finding some deficiencies within himself and his administrative organization which he could not improve on. There were constant symptoms that the quality of the administration was on the downtrend, but Viklav could not point a finger on what the central issue was. He had consulted a couple of wise men in his kingdom, but they were unable to give a complete solution. Their advice had not really helped in improving anything substantially. After knowing about Prabuddh, Viklav asked Paadvik to collect more information about him through his men. The information collected gave Viklav the feeling that Prabuddh was the person who could help him and his kingdom.

Prabuddh would stay on an island with some of his disciples. He had spent years in his spiritual practice and post that, had taken up research in the field of organizational management. His first major work was with a kingdom in the Far East. The kingdom had been nearly destroyed by a massive earthquake, killing the King and his family too. The only royal survivor was a fifteen year old son of the King, who was studying in a distant university when the earthquake struck. Prabuddh worked with the young successor, and helped him recreate the kingdom and bring it back to normalcy in a short span of time. Later, Prabuddh spent time in the University that Paadvik had visited, helping it raise its standard. He also worked for an Ayurveda research centre, helped the team there establish best practices taking it to great strides. Prabuddh would take up assignments only if he liked them; otherwise he was happy being in his own den, spending time with his disciples and of course, with himself.

Viklav and Queen 'Nikasha' decided to visit the island and request Prabuddh to be their advisor. They took up a journey by sea. It took them seven days to reach the island. They were very impressed with the way the Ashram and the local management on the tiny piece of land was handled. To their pleasant surprise, Prabuddh readily accepted the invitation, and promised to come in a month later for an initial period of at least three months.

Viklav and Paadvik had come to the dock to welcome Prabuddh to the Paryaakul kingdom. Prabuddh had started his journey a week earlier, and Viklav was informed the earlier evening that Prabuddh would arrive in Praami anytime in the morning. As Viklav and Paadvik, seated in the chariot were busy discussing administrative issues, Paadvik suddenly noticed a ship moving fast in their direction leaving all the fishing boats behind. He instructed a few of the soldiers to move towards the dock. As the soldiers walked towards the dock, the cart drivers noticed them and suddenly went quiet. They also started looking in the direction of the ship coming in, and realized that some visitors were coming in. As the ship came in closer, the royal chariot also moved at a rapid pace towards the dock. Leaving the already surprised cart drivers in a shocked state, the King and the Minister got down from the chariot, and started looking in the direction of the arriving ship. The ship took some time to anchor in, and to have the only passenger de-boarded. A couple of soldiers went in the ship and helped Prabuddh to walk down the ladder to the platform. As soon as he was on ground, Viklav took a few quick steps to reach to him and greeted him with the traditional feet touching as a mark of request.

"Welcome to Paryaakul," he said with hands joined. Paadvik followed suit.

"Thank you," Prabuddh said with a smile. Looking around the beach, the trees behind, and the hills on one side of the beach, he said, "This appears to be a very beautiful place. I had heard about your state. I am very happy to be here."

Paadvik was seeing him for the first time. Prabuddh had a muscular built, and was of average height. He had almost entirely greyed hair and beard. His voice was gentle, but strong. But what left the biggest impression on Paadvik was Prabuddh's face. His smile was so serene; it appeared as if there could be nothing more pure than it. His eyes had a mysterious feel, as if they were taking control of the person facing them. Paadvik was completely captivated by those eyes. He did not realize whether or not he said something to Prabuddh. By the time he could get back to his normal level of awareness, he noticed that he was accompanying his King and Mitr Prabuddh in the royal chariot which was moving fast towards the palace.

The Story of a Kingdom

"Y ou can call me just Prabuddh," Mitr Prabuddh said with the serene smile on his face, as he could see that Viklav found it difficult to choose the right words to address him. "Let us do away with all formality. We are now just two people trying to sort out issues with a system. Let us be peers in the process. I will also address you by your name, unless you have a problem."

Viklav was surprised to some extent, but agreed to the concept.

"Ok, Prabuddh," he said uttering every word with a conscious effort, though his mind had not fully accepted addressing someone of Prabuddh's stature by his name.

"That is good," Prabuddh said, as he rested on the wooden chair in the garden of the guest house in the royal palace. He continued, "We did speak briefly when you visited my Ashram a month ago. Can you now tell me what exactly is troubling you? What is the matter you are concerned with? Please give as much detail as possible."

"Yes, surely," Viklav said.

It was late morning and was the first formal meeting between Prabuddh and Viklav. Prabuddh, who had arrived in Paryaakul the earlier morning, was quite tired from his journey and needed some rest to refresh him. He slept peacefully in the night and woke up at sunrise as was his daily routine. He went for a walk across the banks of the river flowing adjacent to the royal palace. He then meditated for a while. He felt he was now ready to start working. So, he requested the attendant in the guest house to give a message to the King inviting him to the guest house for a discussion. The King was very keen to start the process as well, and came over in no time. He enquired whether Prabuddh had found the arrangements to his satisfaction and whether he could get sound sleep. Prabuddh thanked him for the arrangement in the guest house which he was completely satisfied with, and then quickly moved the conversation to the main agenda. As the attendants served breakfast of freshly cut fruits, Viklav started narrating his thoughts.

"I do not know if I can express everything properly in words. But the whole thing is that I am unhappy with the way my kingdom is run. I took over the reins of Paryaakul about 20 years back. My father suddenly passed away due to a snake bite when on a hunting tour in the wild. I was not exposed to the administration until then. I had spent several years acquiring knowledge on various subjects, and developing war expertise. Later, I had developed interest in history and had taken up reading ancient text, large part of which was how kingdoms were managed in the past. With the sudden death of my father, I became the King. I had certain ideas of how I wanted to run this

13

state. I wanted to make it a model state. To make that happen, I put in everything. I worked day and night for the welfare of the citizens of this state. For some reasons, during the tenures of my grandfather and my father, our kingdom had lost its past reputation. Things had gone downhill. I do not really remember seeing my grandfather, but my father was never interested in being a ruler. His interest was music, and he worked like a part-time King. I changed this completely. I became a full-time King, and actually much more than that. I wanted to see change. Change was my passion, and I did succeed in raising the standard of our folks. The effort I put in the first ten years helped me achieve all that I wanted to. Then, my ambitions grew. The kingdom next to ours was in a bad shape. The people were dying of starvation, and a large number of people from there were constantly moving in our state as refugees. The King of that state was an idiot and was neither aware nor bothered of what was happening. We did welcome the refugees initially and helped them settle in. However, as the number grew, I thought it would be better if we could take over the administration of that state, and help the people there live better lives in their own state. So, I invaded that kingdom. It was an easy victory, and I attached that state to ours. From thereon, similar expansion happened in two other adjoining states. Paryaakul kingdom now became significantly large. But something went wrong from there. Several events have taken place in the last five years or so, which tell me that I have not been able to reach the level of welfare for my people that I wished to reach. The new states added have not been anywhere close to the standard we had reached ten years back when the state was small. The standard in the original state also has been going down. Few months back, I visited two of the attached states, only to find that we are still far off from the model state I had in my mind. When I came back, I found that in my absence the administration in the Headquarters had collapsed.

The Council of Ministers was waiting for me to take key decisions. Several initiatives which could have been taken were not taken. On seeing this, I lost my sleep and started working more than ever.

"It was not that over this period, we were only failing. There were number of initiatives we took, and many of them were successful. But none of them gave us sustained success. The administration would lose focus over the particular matter in course of time, and as soon as that happened, all that was achieved earlier would disappear.

"I do not know how to deal with this. I have given the prime years of my life for the sake of this kingdom. I have sacrificed time that my family deserved from me, time that my personal interests demanded of me, for the sake of this kingdom. But as I see it now, I am at Square zero, exactly where I started from, and all these years have been a waste. I need your guidance. Please help me. Tell me what to do, how to deal with this problem."

Prabuddh silently listened and tried to capture as much as possible, through his ears as well as eyes. "Viklav," he said, "I understood the overall problem. Do not worry; this is not something we cannot repair." His speech was slow, assuring and strong. "While speaking, you made a reference to the Council of Ministers. At times, you also used the word 'we'. Can you explain how the administration is structured, who are the key people, and what is your opinion about them?"

"We have a Council of Ministers, with each Minister leading a specific department. In every department, there is a team of people working under the Minister. Every department has a general administration team to look at overall matters and state wise teams to look at matters specific to individual states. These teams are led by managers reporting into the Minister. My general assessment of each of these people is that they are very good in terms of their knowledge and experience. It is just that they are not responsive. They do not take initiatives. They are not in control. I attempted several things to change this. I changed people in some key positions. I swapped some people. I also had some people to leave the administration. But somehow, none of the things worked. And I do not know what to do about this."

Prabuddh's mind was in action, trying to put things in perspective. He was also constantly analyzing Viklav's body language and his expressions. He noted that Viklav had a strong passion for the work that he was doing. He would never need a push to do stuff. He was a self-starter. He also had a deep source of energy that helped him work long hours. He was learned, and had lot of knowledge across fields, including practical knowledge. He was very committed to his job.

In the meantime, Viklav continued to speak, and narrated several incidents where he felt his administration could have done much better. One such incident was when a cyclone had destroyed few villages on the coast. Since a warning was received from the weather department, necessary action was taken in time, and thousands of people shifted to temporary relief camps before the cyclone. There was not a single life lost. However, after the cyclone receded, they were all sent home. Their homes, farms and livestock were destroyed, and there was nothing to eat. By the time the administration captured this information, and sent food stock to the affected areas, seventy people had died due to starvation.

In a second incident, since there was an outbreak of a contagious disease, the Health department personnel went house to house distributing preventive medicine. During the same period, officers from the Agriculture department were also going house to house distributing seeds and fertilizers. It was later observed that the two campaigns could easily have been combined saving cost and time.

In a third incident, a warning was received from the Agriculture department that the kingdom's wheat stock was getting over soon. The warning came only when the stock had reached one month's level. The kingdom produced very small quantities of wheat, and normally imported wheat from a distant state, which took four months to arrive from that state. Stock was available in a nearby state as well, with a travel time of two months, but it was more expensive. But given the shortage position, the state had to buy the expensive wheat and also ration distribution of existing stock to public. A similar problem had occurred four times in six years.

As Viklav was narrating the incidents he could remember, a sudden smile appeared on Prabuddh's face. It was not his normal smile, but a smile indicating he felt really happy about something. Viklav was surprised. He was narrating some incidents, which in his opinion indicated a very sad state of affairs. He did not expect a reaction of that kind from Prabuddh.

"I am sorry," said Prabuddh, realizing that Viklav had found this very strange. "I understand your point," he continued, "The events display complete mis-management. However, something that I observed made me very happy. Particularly, I noticed two qualities – care for people, and commitment. I can see that the administration is really concerned for the citizens, and is ready to take extra efforts for their benefit. This settles one very fundamental question in my mind." He paused or a few seconds. "Yes, commitment and concern is not enough. Things have to be planned and executed better. But if the concern or commitment were missing, nothing else would have worked. Hence, I felt happy to some extent. The way you safeguarded people from the cyclone, or distributed preventive medicine, I can see what you meant by a 'model state' that you have in your mind."

"Yes, we are very concerned," Viklav said in a sarcastic tone indicating disagreement, "but what is the use? If seventy people die on account of negligence, what do I do with that concern? My team took extra effort to ensure the stock of wheat lasted till we had replenishment. But why could not they put in some effort to ensure this situation did not arise in the first place? These things are extremely frustrating. I need your help. I have talked about these issues several times with the team members. Nothing has worked. I need your help in talking to them. Please educate them. Train them. I do not know how to do this. Please help." His anger suddenly changed to exasperation.

Prabuddh's smile was back to its normal serene nature. "I understand your feelings," he said softly, "I have got a good idea of what is happening, and why it bothers you. But do not worry. There is never a problem which does not have a solution. In fact, the solution is embedded in the problem itself. You do not need to create a solution; you only need to discover it. We have discussed symptoms of the problem. Let us now try to define it properly. Then, we will look at discovering the solution and implementing it. I would like to spend some time by myself going over the entire discussion we had now. Let us meet again in the evening. Let us talk then."

"Sure," Viklav had recovered from his frustrated self. "I will see you in the evening," he said.

The Bitter Medicine

P rabuddh was sitting in a meeting room in the main ministerial section of the administrative office. He was reflecting on the discussion in the morning and the analysis he had done after the morning meeting. As he sat with his eyes closed trying to firm up his thoughts, Viklav arrived in the room.

"Good evening," he greeted Prabuddh, "Sorry for the delay. I had to deal with some urgent matters. Sorry to keep you waiting," he said as he took his seat.

The room went into a silent mode as Prabuddh tried to gather the right words.

"Viklav," he said, "I have spent the whole day trying to put the problem on hand in the right perspective. As I said in the morning, proper definition of the problem is very important and could also be the most difficult part. I think I have got to a clear definition of what is going wrong."

"That makes me really happy," Viklav exclaimed, "So, how do you want to go about meeting the Council of Ministers? Do you want to meet them one by one, or as a group? When should I fix the meetings?"

Prabuddh shook his head. With a smile, he said, "This is not the way to go about. The first thing is that we cannot hurry with this process. The second is that I am not going to speak to your Ministers."

Viklav was in shock. He had already started planning for meetings between Prabuddh and the Ministers. He did not know how to react to what Prabuddh had just said.

"Viklav," Prabuddh said very slowly, "As I said, problem definition is the most important part of the process. You and I have to be very clear on what exactly is the issue that we are trying to resolve. Once this is done, the rest will not be as difficult. What in your opinion is the problem that we have to work on?"

Viklav thought for a minute. "It is some issue with the administration team," he said, "with the Council of Ministers. I do not know what exactly, but there is something that stops them sometimes from doing even a common sense job."

"Defining that something is critical, Viklav. You yourself said that the people are generally good. But there is something missing. Now, the issue is that there are ten or twenty or fifty people who are all good, but yet are not performing on expected lines. So, it cannot be that something has gone wrong individually with each of them. Rather, it appears there is something missing more generally. There is something wrong in the environment. The environment of an organization is defined by its culture. There is a cultural deficiency in this administration."

"Ok," Viklav responded, "probably this is the thing that I

could see missing, but could not specify. Culture could very well be the gap. But Prabuddh, why do you say you will not speak to the Ministers? Are not they the ones running the administration? Is not a cultural gap their duty to fix?"

"It is. But, it is not primarily their duty."

"So whose duty is it?"

"Yours, Viklav."

Viklav was stunned. "Do you mean that the problem is with me, rather than the administration?" He appeared completely disappointed.

"Viklav, Do not get me wrong. Please listen carefully to what I am now going to say. First of all, you have invited me to your kingdom with a specific objective, which is that you expect me to help you. That is my primary job. If the way to help you is by saying something that may hurt you, I do not mind doing that. My primary responsibility is towards the task I have accepted, and not towards making you feel nice.

"Secondly, I have no doubts whatsoever, about your passion to make this state a model state. I can also see that you have put in your life and soul into this journey. But probably, knowingly or unknowingly, consciously or sub-consciously, you have allowed certain deficiencies to creep in the system of this administration. I would like if you could consciously think about this, and take corrective actions wherever you feel a need. There are two possibilities I see. One is that, there are certain qualities in your DNA which are not fully appropriate for the organization, and need to be relooked at. The second thing is that there are certain qualities in your DNA which are very appropriate for the organization, but these things have not been transferred to the DNA of the organization. Hence, the organization does not work

21

in line with those qualities unless you make it work that way. In both these cases, the primary work is at your end.

"The third and a very important thing is that a system can be successful only if it is a self-sufficient and sustainable. If it is not self-sufficient, a lot of energy is consumed to keep it running. Systems in nature are always self-sufficient; they power themselves. Look at the mighty river flowing next to this palace. Do you need to do anything to keep it running? Water coming from the mountains accumulates, keeps flowing from the highs towards the sea in a continuous manner. In doing so, it also creates an entire eco-system within and around it, needing no artificial intervention. The river is full of life. Different kinds of organisms live and thrive in it. But do they need to be fed by someone? No, because there is food available for all of them. But look at the artificial fish tank you have created in the garden. I saw it in the morning. It has some very beautiful fish with stunning shapes and colours. But it is not a self-sufficient system. You have to constantly feed the fish. I am sure you will also have to regularly clean and maintain the tank. So, a lot of energy is spent in keeping the system running. In case you forget to feed the fish for a few days, they will die, because they are dependent on you for everything. Apart from being self-sufficient, the system also needs to be sustainable. Once developed, it should run constantly. Just like the river. It would have been flowing for several centuries, and will keep flowing for many more centuries to come. We will need to develop systems that will not depend on you or anyone else for getting solutions or for maintaining solutions implemented. They should be spontaneous and continuous. If I speak to your Ministers and convince them of how the administration should run, we are breaking the rule of self-sufficiency. I will not be here after a few days or weeks. You will continue as the King. The people should do things because you want them to do those, rather than me wanting. This will be the first step towards self-sufficiency and sustainability. Even when you direct them, the direction should not only specify the task, but the thought behind the task. So that slowly, they absorb the thought and start working on their own. This is where the system becomes completely self-sufficient and sustainable. It becomes spontaneous and continuous, and you should withdraw at this stage. Your job is not to give all answers, but ask the right questions. If you give all the answers, your people will become like fish in your fish tank. They will depend on you for everything, which they should not. Similarly, if I bring in the change, you will depend on me. My job is to change you, your thoughts, your approach, and you have to bring in change in the rest. This will be a sustainable, self-sufficient model.

"Viklav, now let us do one exercise. I want you to write down on a piece of paper, the names of key departments in your administration. Then, organize them in a tier structure, so that tier one represents the core departments, and the last tier the peripheral ones."

Viklav was lost in thoughts. He had not expected Prabuddh to say what he did. He had thought that Prabuddh would become a teacher for his Ministers, and work closely with them training them on their deficiencies. But it appeared now that Viklav himself had to become the student, and with good reasoning behind it, which was difficult to challenge. He tried to stop the thought process to focus on doing the exercise that Viklav had asked him to do. He asked an attendant for some paper and a pen, which was provided. He thought for a while, and started scribbling on the paper.

"This is how I would categorize our departments," Viklav said as he presented the paper to Prabuddh. Prabuddh looked at the paper with deep attention. This is what Viklav had written:

> Tier 1: Security, Agriculture, Commerce
>
> Tier 2: Finance, People, Health
>
> Tier 3: Education, Civil Infrastructure
>
> Tier 4: Religion, Art, Foreign Affairs

Prabuddh smiled. He said, "I agree with this grouping. The way it works is that the core, represented by tier one relates to life, food, and income – the most basic functions. Tier two functions provide support to the tier one functions, and so on, going up to the last tier. Correct?"

"Yes, I used the same logic."

"Now tell me, if you have to use different degrees of delegation for each of the tier levels, which tier will have the least delegation?"

"Of course, tier one. The core is what needs my maximum attention."

"Perfect. While I agree with the grouping you have done based on core and support nature of functions, where in this tier structure have you provided for sustainability and self-sufficiency?"

Viklav did not have an answer. He was confused.

"Viklav, you have got your prioritization right. But…." Prabuddh paused for a while and pulled a second sheet of paper. He started drawing something on it, and continued speaking as he drew. "There has to be another force which will keep the prioritization intact and the methods to deal with them consistent, automatic, and self-correcting. This force is called culture. Hence, my grading is like this." He handed the paper to Viklav.

Prabuddh had drawn circles which appeared as below:

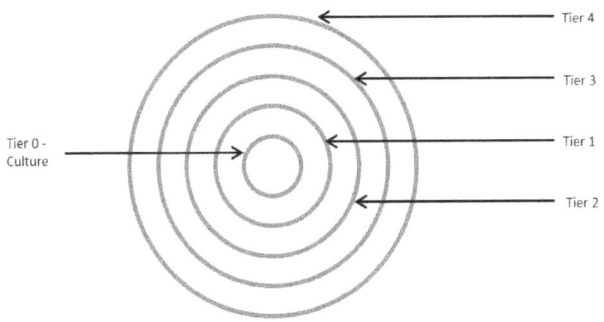

"Culture is right at the core of entire operations, it is even more core than the core functions you identified. You can say it is at tier zero," Prabuddh said as Viklav studied the diagram in front of him. "On a long term basis, culture is the most important function for an organization setup."

"So why is it at tier zero? Why not instead call it tier one, and the core identified by me be put at tier two?"

"Because culture has a unique feature. It is the most important thing which by itself means nothing. This resembles what zero does in mathematics. By itself, zero has no value. But if it stands next to any number, it can multiply its value ten times. Secondly, the way you drew the structure, the core functions were at the centre, while the support functions were at the periphery. Culture in that sense is not an operational function at all. But it is a core function. So I call it a 'core support' function. To show its unique importance, I call its placement as tier zero."

Viklav nodded.

"The problem is that culture is never given adequate importance as an activity. It usually gets created by itself rather than a special effort being made to create it. This is fine, if the right culture is being created. A special effort is definitely required to constantly monitor whether the right culture is prevailing and if not, to take necessary action to install the right culture. While culture has an organization-wide presence, I put it at the centre to indicate that this is one activity that can never be delegated."

Viklav was completely taken aback by the last sentence. Prabuddh said it very normally, in a matter-of-fact way, but Viklav found the statement really strong.

"You are surprised, right?" Prabuddh continued, "We all know that delegation is a key requirement for improvement in efficiency. But so as to ensure that delegation in other areas works fine, culture is one area that should always be centralized. By creating the right culture, the systems will become automatic and self-correcting. Hence, the system will itself decide what the right amount of delegation is for every other function."

"Prabuddh, what you are saying makes a lot of sense. But, a part of my brain is also confused. What exactly is culture? Let us accept for some time that my administration has a cultural deficiency. My question is how a better culture would have prevented occurrence of some of the events that I narrated?"

"I can understand. Your question is also very important. Culture, is simply the way a group of people does things. Let me give an example. A few minutes back, you asked the attendant to give us some papers. The exact language you used was 'Can you please give us some blank papers to write and a couple of pens?' Your words were kind and respectful. Your voice and tone had lot of warmth. Your facial expressions were very pleasant, and you addressed the person by his name. So many cultural traits came out of this small communication. You demonstrated several emotions - respect, kindness, affection, care…. all coming from a King towards an attendant. The care with which you conversed with the attendant – where and how did you learn this way of speaking?"

"I…. I am not sure. This is how I always do it….. at least most of the times," Viklav said, "Umm…. probably my parents taught this. But, seriously, I am not sure."

"Fair enough. That is what culture is. It is there without you knowing it is there and how it has reached there. Tell me, do your wife and children behave in a similar way?"

"Yes," Viklav said very firmly.

"So this is your family culture. Now, tell me, does every person part of your administration team behave in a similar way with every person they deal with?"

"I think so," Viklav said after thinking for a while.

"Note the differences in your responses, Viklav. You are very sure that your family members have the same behaviour patterns with attendants as you have. But you are not exactly sure that your administration team would exhibit similar patterns."

"I have never paid attention, frankly. Hence, I am not sure."

"Exactly. That is the problem. Culture never gets adequate attention. If you bring in the right culture in your organization, and you have for assumption sake fifty people in your organization, then those fifty people are like fifty Viklavs who will respond to situations in a way very similar to yours. But if

Viklav and the organization have two separate sets of cultures, the organization will never work the way you expect it to work, unless you personally intervene in every matter."

Viklav's face turned bright. It was as if he had suddenly seen light while walking through a dark tunnel. He imagined all his Ministers and other staff doing things the way he himself would have done. Now he could see what Prabuddh meant.

Prabuddh observed that Viklav had started seeing sense in what he was saying. He gave Viklav a couple of minutes of silence, so that the thoughts could penetrate better into him.

"Now, let us talk about what the right culture could have done to the incidents you narrated," he continued. "Let us start with the cyclone issue. What do you think went wrong here?"

"The people did not do the job to the end. They did one part of it, and did it brilliantly well. But the next part was managed pathetically."

"Correct. I see two issues here. First, I think there was a communication issue. The seniors told the team to do the task in a particular way and they followed the instructions. I do not believe that the team that did one part of the job very well could fail on delivering the other part, unless they were asked to focus only on one part. So, the communication from the top was an issue. Secondly, the monitoring of the job was a complete failure. Once a job is undertaken, it is important for the leadership to track the status until it reaches a logical conclusion. Both the wrongs are cultural issues.

"Now the next incident, the one in which two departments invested in duplicate efforts. This problem was clearly a coordination problem. This is very common. It is like the eyes not knowing what the hands are doing. The administration is not an integrated system. This is completely a cultural issue.

"Now let us look at the last incident, where you ran out of stock of wheat number of times. Who, in your opinion, was the culprit here?"

"It was the Agriculture Minister. It was his responsibility."

"Ok. If you were in his place, what would you have done?"

"I would have put a process in place whereby on a regular basis, say weekly, I would get a report of the stock available."

"So, is there no such system right now in place?"

"There is. But when we investigated, I was told that wrong data was being reported."

"So this is not the Minister's mistake. Even if you were in his place, the data would still be wrong."

"But the Minister should have been more vigilant, especially after this problem having been repeated. He could have done physical checks rather than relying only on reports."

"Agreed. So, the reason was not a personal failure, but a process issue. Process is a large part of culture. So, overall, if the culture was right, all these issues could have been avoided."

Viklav nodded, though it appeared as if he did not know why.

"Viklav, now if I say, on all the three matters we discussed, in your capacity as the King, you have not worked seriously enough, do you agree with me?"

"How can you say that, Prabuddh? As soon as I learnt

of the deaths after the cyclone, I was immediately at the place myself. I did not move from there till I ensured every household had food stock delivered sufficient for two days, and the supply process was in place for the next few weeks. I also put people on the job to ensure the reconstruction of houses started immediately. I stayed there for two nights and then had a regular follow up of the status on ground. On the second incident, I did not really act because no action was required. But on the wheat stock issue, it was me who got into sourcing and negotiating wheat supplies, and deciding the rationing mechanism. I also followed up on the status until regular wheat supplies resumed."

"Understood," Prabuddh did not appear affected by the angry outburst from Viklav, "You did work seriously. But you worked on corrective actions. Did you do any preventive work? Let me reword my earlier sentence and say that you did not work seriously enough on the culture part. Will you agree now?"

Viklav had nothing to say. He kept looking at Prabuddh.

"You put in your heart and soul into the corrective actions. That is your nature. But in doing so, you created additional dependence on yourself. You did what was the need of the hour. But did you put in any effort in creating fifty Viklavs in the system, who would ensure that the problems would not recur, and if that they did recur, those fifty Viklavs would deal with the matter themselves rather than waiting for you to act?

"You said the Agriculture Minister was not vigilant enough. But have you demonstrated to him the need to be vigilant? After the shortage problem had occurred thrice, did you ask of him a plan to ensure it will not repeat a fourth time? When the cyclone occurred, were you taking reports from the concerned Minister on the state of affairs till everything was smooth again? By doing so, you would have demonstrated the importance you give to these matters. Possibly, the incidents could have been avoided. Not only that, the DNA of your people itself would have been reprogrammed over time, understanding how they are expected to respond in such situations. But instead of also taking the more effective step of setting a culture, you took only the more effortful step of being on the ground when the things had gone wrong. In a way, you demonstrated that you care more for the corrective action rather than the preventive action, and this has effectively now become the culture of this administration."

"My administration team has members with a significant seniority. If they will not do a job till I do a review with them, what's the point in having them? They have to work on their own."

"Can you apply the same rule when it comes to taking corrective action? At that stage the job becomes so critical that you have to be on the ground. Then, why not be equally concerned as regards preventive action? The expectation you have from your people is correct. But if that expectation is not being met, you are left with only two alternatives – first, be on the ground taking corrective actions whenever there is a failure, or second, do the reviews regularly so that the people pick up the right culture, and overtime, you can withdraw. I suspect that they are not meeting the expectation because they have absorbed the prevalent culture, and the prevalent culture is that everything is led by you. Change the culture and you will see that the people change. Remember, culture is something that is not linked to genetics. It simply relates to upbringing. If for assumption sake, you pick up two new born babies who have exactly the same DNA, and they are adopted by two different families with vastly different cultures, the two will pick the cultures of their respective families irrespective of their original constitution being exactly the same."

Viklav was completely speechless. He was experiencing two contradicting emotions towards Prabuddh at the same time – that of anger and gratitude. He felt angry because he was being told something that he did not like; he felt thankful because he was being told something that he had never thought of before. He felt angry because the flaw was found at his end; he felt thankful because he would have never found the flaw had he not been made to look within. He felt angry because the problem appeared to have emanated from him; he felt thankful because the solution also appeared to be within him. While the emotions were fighting each other, a sudden thought came to his mind. He had a doubt he needed to clarify. He asked, "Why are these problems being experienced only now? I never faced them in my initial tenure. I have not changed over the years. So, why has the situation changed?"

"Viklav, your kingdom has grown over the years. Few years back, when it was small, it was possible for you to be almost everywhere, every time. You could sense a problem even before it erupted. Even if a problem did erupt, its magnitude would be much smaller. Now, with a much larger kingdom and an increased size of the administration, you cannot be as close to every problem as you used to be earlier. This is exactly why you need fifty Viklavs in the system, so that every problem could be dealt with in your style. This can happen only through culture building. You can easily feed the fish in your fish tank every day. Can you do the same with respect to the fish in the river? No. You will need to create self-sustaining, self-powering systems to run a large organization."

Viklav sat quietly reflecting over the entire discussion. It had taken a completely different direction as against the expectation with which he had started it. He closed his eyes and tried to focus his thoughts. Prabuddh allowed him the time. As Viklav opened his eyes a couple of minutes later, Prabuddh very calmly said, "I can understand what you are going through. What I have shared with you is a paradigm shift for you. Think on it. Give yourself time to absorb all that we have discussed. Once you think that you have digested everything, once you feel synchronized with me on the definition of the problem, let us meet again. I do not wish to hurry up on the process. Actually, this is the most important part of the process. Once this is done, the rest will follow a logical route from where we stand to where we want to reach."

"But what exactly will that route be?"

"I would have liked to talk on this only once you tell me that you completely understand and agree with what I have said. But I will give you a brief description of the process. First, I am going to work with you and only with you. Getting the culture right is your responsibility. As I said, it cannot be delegated. Second, I will try to share with you the theoretical knowledge on culture in an organization. We will have regular sessions. It will not be something that you have not learnt earlier, you would know most of it. I have only organized it better, so it is easy to grasp. Third, you can share with me your real time problems or issues. We, together, will try to find culture solutions to those problems, which you will implement. We will try to relate every problem to the conceptual knowledge on culture. We have to work on two areas – one, areas, where you personally need to do some cultural adjustments. You will have to be open for a self-assessment in these areas. Two, areas, where the culture you follow personally, and the one that the organization follows, are different. In the first set of areas, you will have to work on changing yourself. In the second, you will have to work on aligning the organization's culture to yours. Once you start realizing that Viklav is changing, and more and more Viklavs are appearing in the system, and that you need less and less of my inputs, my job will be done. It surely will not happen overnight. Change takes its own time. We should meet once a week, and the balance period will be for you to absorb and implement what we discuss. We will have to commit our focus to this activity and give it due importance. It is best not to tell people that we are going to change the culture of this place. Culture creation can never be talked or written. It can only work through demonstration. Talking and writing cannot create culture, but only reinforce it."

"Wow…. That sounds like a mission, and a secret one," Viklav found a way of getting himself back to his normal self. "Thank you Prabuddh. You have shared a good amount of wisdom with me over a short period of time. Yes, I definitely need some time to absorb all that you have presented before me. I do not think I will trouble you over the next few days. I will come back to you once I am through this process."

"Sure," a smiling Prabuddh said.

"The attendants will be at your service. Please do let me know if you need anything. Please do make yourself comfortable. Our attendants will be happy to take you around the city, if you wish. We have some lovely temples and some nice spots where you can enjoy nature's beauty."

"Thank you. The attendants are very helpful and I will use their services where required. I look forward to seeing you again soon, so we could commence our next steps."

"See you Prabuddh."

Section II

The Journey

The Leader's Baby

"Thank you Viklav. Thanks for agreeing with me," said Prabuddh. It was almost a week since their last meeting. Viklav had requested Prabuddh for a meeting the earlier evening. Prabuddh had suggested if they could meet in the morning instead. So, Viklav actually joined Prabuddh for his morning walk by the river. They had walked some distance, when Viklav spoke saying he is in agreement to the method that Prabuddh wanted to employ.

"It is I who has to thank you for showing me a completely different direction," Viklav said, "Something I had never thought of."

"Being open to a completely new idea is not easy. That is the reason I thanked you," responded Prabuddh, "Your readiness to entertain this idea and to work on it is worth appreciating."

"I did a lot of thinking on it. In a way, I tried my best to find a reason to reject the idea, and I failed. Then it struck me that this is the correct path, this is the path I should take. I felt as if I wanted to construct a building and was focused on the roof, or the walls, doors and windows. You wanted me to look at the foundation. As soon as that thought arrived, I knew I had to do it. There was no time to waste at all; I had to do it right away."

"That is a good metaphor. The foundation is the most important and at the same time the most hidden part of a structure. Just like culture. The solution to any problem has a layered structure. You can get various solutions to the same problem, with each solution being appropriate to one particular layer. The most critical part is determining the layer at which you want to create the solution. The deeper the layer, that much sustainable and spontaneous the solution will be. Going by your example of a building, the top most part of the building is the roof. The roof top is based on the roof structure. The roof structure is based on the walls. The walls themselves are a structure built brick by brick, and in turn are based on the foundation. Culture is the deepest layer in an organization. If you solve the problem at the level of this layer, you will never have to relook at the same problem again. But mind you, solving problems at this layer can take a lot of time. It may need patience and persistence. It is very similar to how the foundation of a structure can take a lot of time. But, it is worth to invest time in problem solving at the core layer, so that the problem does not repeat, and overtime the number of problems goes down."

"If that is the case, why I have not heard about culture creation as a tool for problem solving before? No one has even referred to this concept."

"Viklav, the human mind has its own way of working. We do work to derive satisfaction from doing it. The satisfaction comes by seeing results coming out of the work put in. Results are more easily visible when work is put in the more shallow layers. Deeper the layer you work on, the immediate visibility of results is that much lesser. But, the results do come after a while. They come in a way that no one notices them as a special occurrence. It appears as if they are coming on their own. More importantly, the results are sustained over a long period of time. Given this, people always like to work on the areas which give quick visible results rather than those which have a longer gestation period and when the results come, it appears they have come on their own rather than due to the effort the person has put in. Once you get used to working on the periphery, moving towards the core can become scary. Culture is right there, at the core. Right at the centre."

"......at Tier zero," Viklav said spontaneously, as both of them started laughing.

"Correct. Further, these mind games occur at the sub-conscious level, without we consciously knowing them. So, when you get to know that wheat stock has depleted, you see the problem like an enemy who has invaded your state. You see only that part of the problem which needs immediate action. But there is a part of the problem which is like a potential enemy, miles away from you today. You need to start working on this part of the problem also, and you need to do it now. You need to study what this potential enemy is like, what is his size, what is the potential strategy he will adopt. You have to put in effort to ensure he never thinks of declaring war on you, and if he does, you are prepared for it. Focusing on the enemy at your doorstep makes you take some quick fire steps that give you satisfaction, because they show results. But if you do not work on the potential enemy today, you will have to put in similar effort years later, if and when he becomes a real enemy, knocking at your doors."

"Understood. I can relate to this. In case of the wheat shortage issue, I have worked on the current enemy only. I am still to work on the potential one."

Viklav got thinking on the concept of dealing with the potential enemy. He went silent. Prabuddh did not want to disturb his thought process. He rather increased his pace of walking, and Viklav matched him up without even realizing it. In a few minutes, they were back to the palace. Viklav accompanied Prabuddh to the guest house. They sat in the garden as the attendants served fresh tender coconut water. Both were thirsty from the walk, so they emptied their glasses quickly. Prabuddh went inside the guest house and came out bringing some sheets of paper which he placed on the table. The attendants had brought in some ripe bananas and a warm freshly cooked porridge. The duo started enjoying the breakfast.

"Viklav," Prabuddh said as he was done with a banana, "now that we have crossed one hurdle in our process, that of understanding the problem accurately, I want to introduce you to certain concepts around culture. I will not tell you anything new, but I will arrange it in a structured and scientific manner, so it is easy for you to comprehend and absorb." He took a sheet of paper from the table and kept it in front of Viklav. There was some matter written on it neatly in beautiful hand writing. "These are some of the basic concepts about culture," he said. Prabuddh started reading the page. It contained the following:

CULTURE: BASIC CONCEPTS

1.	The 'How?' of things
2.	Automatic
3.	Continuous
4.	Top driven
5.	Programmable
6.	Dynamic

"We have discussed some of these concepts in our earlier discussions. We will anyways speak on all, even at the cost of repetition. It is important to take an all-round view of the matter on hand. Let us start with the first point.

"Culture is the 'way of life' of a group of people, meaning the way they do things. It consists primarily of values, beliefs, and habits. It explains the 'how' of things. For example, when you read this sheet, how do you read it? You read it left to right or right to left? Top to down or bottom to up? The method you follow is nothing but your culture. One 'how' can lead to multiple related 'how's, both vertically and horizontally. Let us say we are talking about how to make porridge. A vertical extension of this could be how to ensure porridge is made in the same way every time. A horizontal extension could be how to serve it or how to wash the plates after it has been consumed. Culture is the sum total of all 'how's. What is visible is the demonstrated culture. What is at the bottom of it is the culture continuity. Going by the same example of porridge making, the 'how' of ensuring that the porridge is always made in the same way is about culture continuity."

Prabuddh picked up the plate of porridge, and started

eating from it. Viklav looked at the sheet and stared at the second point.

"What do you mean by 'automatic'?" he asked.

"Culture is automatic," Prabuddh replied, "It happens by itself. You do not have to think or put an effort to do a particular thing in a particular way. It happens by itself."

"But if I have to get my people to follow a proper process to manage the stock of wheat, it cannot be automatic. Everyone will have to put a lot of effort into it."

"Yes, that is correct. But that is because you are at the culture creation stage. You put in effort now. But once the effort translates into a cultural practice, it becomes automatic. Your people would have been making porridge for centuries. The process of making it would have been passed from generation to generation. They do not have to refer to a document that details how to make porridge. They do not have to ask anyone. The process is a part of life for them. Hence, it is automatic."

Viklav started eating from his plate of porridge. Porridge used to be just porridge for him. What else could it be? But today, in place of porridge, he could see centuries' worth of process sitting in his plate. 'This man can make you look at simple, everyday stuff in a completely different manner,' he thought.

Prabuddh continued speaking, "I have a habit of reciting my daily prayer before going to bed every night. My parents and my Guru put in the effort to create this culture in me. Of course, I put effort from my side. But now, no effort is required. It is completely automatic. I do not need to think about it. I do not need reminders. As soon as I am ready to sleep, I will first say the prayer. It has got registered in my sub-conscious that way."

Viklav nodded indicating that he has understood.

"The third point is that it is continuous," Prabuddh continued, "It is an extension of point two. Since it is automatic, it has to be continuous. Culture is something you do every day, every time, unless of course there are exceptional situations. There cannot be a break in culture. I do my prayer every day. Yes, I have missed it a few times, when the situation was exceptional. For example, few years back, I was seriously ill and bed ridden with high fever for almost a week. I did not say my prayer during that period, I just did not have enough energy to even get up and sit.

"But in normal circumstances, I will not get sleep if I miss the prayer, even if I deliberately give it a miss. So, culture is something that happens every day.

"Culture is always top-driven. That is the next point. It always comes from the leader. It is the leader who defines, implements and demonstrates culture. Let us assume that a leader needs a particular kind of culture, say he wants his team members to greet one another every day in a particular way. He will have to first define what is expected. Then, he will have to implement it through communication of what is expected, measurement to check whether the expectation is being fulfilled, and taking corrective actions where it is not. He will also have to demonstrate the culture expected through his own behaviour. But there are forms of culture which happen without being defined as such, are not necessarily implemented as such, but the demonstration is good enough for the particular behaviour to percolate as culture. This particularly applies to the negative part of culture, which does not require discipline. If a mother wants her child to wake up early every day, she will have to decide at what time she wants the child to wake up, and tell the child so. She will have to herself get up before that time, wake up the child at least initially at that time; she will also have to punish the child

43

if it continues rising late after all this effort. This effort is required because getting up early needs discipline. On the other hand if the mother herself rises late every day, the child will automatically pick up that habit since it is very easy to follow. Hence, whether through the process of definition, implementation and demonstration, or merely through demonstration, it is the leader who sets up culture. A very important point to note is that if the leader defines culture in a particular way, but demonstrates differently, people will always follow what is demonstrated, not what is defined. Say, you as the King take out an order that no one in the administration should speak in a raised voice to one another, irrespective of the situation. This is the definition. But if the King himself shouts at someone, then the demonstration is against the definition. There could be a variant of this situation, where passive demonstration comes into play. Say, a Minister of your kingdom raises his voice on a junior person. You are aware of this but you do not correct the Minister or take action against him. This is passive demonstration contrary to the definition. In such cases, it is quite possible that the demonstrated culture may override the defined one. In this case, the demonstration of culture has actually come from a level other than that of the King. But the King, by not acting on it, has given his acceptance to the culture."

Viklav was deep in thoughts. He was trying to relate this concept to a variety of real life situations he had been through. 'I have to be careful as to what I demonstrate to my people,' he thought to himself, '… and always act on situations I am aware of which are not in line with what I expect.' He then looked up at Prabuddh and said, "This is a very important point. But, what if the wrong behaviour has come from a senior member of the team? It may be difficult to question him, particularly if the matter involved is not of critical importance."

"Viklav, the importance of a matter can be determined only at the time you define the culture. If it was not important, why would you create a cultural practice around it? Once this is done, it has to be implemented in a uniform manner, without considering who is at what level. Remember, once you have decided on the culture, no one can be bigger than it, including you. Let us say you have decided that respect for women is a key matter of culture. Once decided, if someone acts contrary to it, and you do not act, the inaction means the culture that you had defined is no longer there. It has got altered. Actually, more senior the person not following the defined culture, the stronger is the alteration. Since culture comes from top, the leader has the highest influence on it; the second tier of leadership has the next best influence, and so on. So, it is more important to correct culture at the top rather than at the bottom."

Prabuddh paused for a while. He could see that Viklav's mind was on a fast-track mode, going around several spots in his memory, trying to establish what he could have done differently in specific circumstances, and how. He was pleased to notice that this concept had hit Viklav at the right place. He was sure if Viklav would get convinced about it, it would have a major influence on the whole process.

"What's the next point on the list?" Prabuddh asked, although he remembered what was on the list, just to draw Viklav's attention back to the sheet of paper.

Viklav looked at the sheet. "Dynamic," he said.

"And the next one?"

"Programmable. That is the last point."

"The two are related. Culture is dynamic and programmable. It can change and it does change. You had earlier mentioned that the reputation of your kingdom went down during your grandfather's and your father's regime. You changed things and brought improvements after you took over. Later, you also experienced a downtrend. Culture changes, but changes slowly. However, I do not think the change during your tenure was due to an organizational culture change. It was mainly due to your personal charisma and hard work. The embedded culture was the same, but you got better of it at a personal level. Hence, once the distance between you and the last point of administration grew, you experienced a failing organization. The culture which was always there, but was hidden, resurfaced. Anyways, the point is that culture is not a fixed state of affairs. It is a dynamic entity. It can change through conscious action, and also through negligence. It can improve. It can also deteriorate.

"Because it is dynamic, it can be programmed the way you want it to be. You can create a culture of your choice. Definitely, it is not easy to do this. It needs a careful definition of what you want to create, and a persistent and committed effort to bring it to life. Even after creating, it needs regular monitoring and corrective actions to maintain the culture. But the takeaway point is that culture can be created.

"With this, we have completed a description of what culture is and what you can do with it. This is what I wanted to cover today. How did you find the session? What's the key point you observed?"

Viklav thought for a moment. He said, "Actually all the points were important. Culture explains the 'how' part of a task. You can call something as culture only once it becomes automatic and is practiced continuously. Culture is top-driven. It is dynamic and can be changed. But in all of this, the point that made me think the most is that culture is completely leader-driven. The leader creates the culture consciously or sub-consciously. Either through action or through inaction. It is completely the responsibility of the leader. He cannot look at anywhere else other than himself to blame if the right culture is not in place."

"Excellent. Very well captured. Before we close for the day, I wanted to repeat the purpose of culture. We discussed this last week as well. But since I have formally presented the concepts around culture to you today, I thought we will discuss this again. Do you remember why we need culture?"

"Yes," Viklav said in a flash, "Culture makes an organization sustainable and self-sufficient. Spontaneous and continuous."

Prabuddh smiled. He could see the beginning of a new enlightenment. He felt happy that they were on the right track.

Culture
Creation

"**G**ood morning," Viklav said as he and Prabuddh started walking outside the gates of the palace early morning. They were meeting after a week. Viklav had liked the idea of doing the meeting over a morning walk with Prabuddh. It allowed him to be away from his normal environment.

"Good morning Viklav," Prabuddh returned the greetings with a smile.

"What's next on our agenda?" Viklav questioned.

"In our last meeting we went through the conceptual background of culture. Now, we are going to look at culture in terms of its structure. Then, we will discuss the constituents of culture - what traits the right culture is made up of."

"Sure. Prabuddh, I have a couple of points to discuss before we take up this part. Is that fine?"

"Oh, sure. Please feel free to tell me whatever you feel

is important to be discussed."

"The first point is regarding the issue we have been discussing all this while – that of the wheat shortage. Since our last meeting, I have been thinking of how to deal with the issue through the culture route. Earlier, I had almost decided that I would instruct one of my personal team members to visit the stores every week and report the stock value to me directly. But from our discussion, I realized that if I do this, I will be working outside the system put in place to manage this task. It will be against culture setting and will increase dependence on me. So, I decided against it."

"That is excellent, Viklav. You have done the right thing. I am very happy that you have understood the significance of culture."

"So instead I did a meeting with the Agriculture Minister. I told him that the repeated problems have been an issue and they have to be dealt with strongly. Then I asked him to come out with a process that will ensure that the problem does not repeat."

"Superb," Prabuddh was getting increasingly happy.

"Yesterday he came back to me. He has suggested that he will continue with the weekly reporting process for getting inventory data, and he will himself do a monthly physical inspection of the store to ensure he is getting the right data. I thought it was a good idea, but wanted to check with you on what you think about it."

"This is a good beginning. You asked the right question and made him think. But as I said earlier, solutions can be found at different levels, and we have to attempt going to the deepest level possible. The first thing that comes to my mind is what is the logic of deciding the monthly frequency of physical visits?

Why not fortnightly? Why not quarterly? I am not saying monthly frequency is wrong. But let there be proper logic to the decision. Second, how will he ensure he does his monthly task? What is his way of remembering? Which day of the month will he do it? Next, will he give a report to you on a monthly basis as well? How will you ensure that his report to you comes in and gets analyzed? Further up, with respect to the weekly report that the Minister gets, what is the process used to create that report? Who makes it? Is there a quality check of the report before it goes to the Minister?"

Viklav appeared overwhelmed with the barrage of questions fired at him. "But Prabuddh...." he said hesitantly, "if I have to answer all these questions, how will this create culture? Will I not make the system more dependent on me?"

Prabuddh smiled. "See, as far as getting the report at your end and analyzing it is concerned; this task has to be managed at your end only. It signifies your commitment to the process. As far as what happens between the Minister and the stock of wheat, you are supposed to ask these questions of the Minister. By asking these questions, you will be educating him on how to think. You are not supposed to give answers to him, but you are supposed to ask the right questions. Only once you get convincing answers to your questions, will you get the confidence that the process will work. If he does not have the answer, let him go back and get it. This is how culture will be created."

"But asking him how he will remember that he has to do a physical site inspection will be like stretching it too far...... I mean he is a senior resource."

"No, I do not think so. You are only trying to make the process full-proof. And you have had failures. Repeated ones. Let me now ask the same question of you. How will you ensure to check that you have got the monthly report and it is analyzed?"

"I remember such things. I have a strong memory."

"I am sure you do. But that is not good enough. You cannot rely only on memory. You need a better way which will allow you to remember."

"So what should I do?"

"Just like I do not want you to give any answers to your Minister, I will also not like to give an answer to you. You think and tell me what will be a better way." Prabuddh paused for a moment. "Viklav, I can understand that asking this question to the Minister appears silly. It can be embarrassing for the Minister and for you too. But this embarrassment is much better than you being embarrassed before lacs of citizens."

There was a minute of silence.

"Ok. I will do it. I will ask these questions of the Minister," Viklav said, "with regard to ensuring the report comes to me...... I think the best way is to make a note in my notebook."

"Which is good...., but you will also have to inculcate the habit of going through the notebook regularly. It happens quite often that people write and then forget to read what they have written. This tool of writing things down is called the checklist. There are two important parts of it – the list and the check. It is important to put everything important in a list and it is equally important to check the list regularly."

Viklav smiled. "Yes," he said, "I will definitely do this."

"Now that we are talking about how to create culture..... I need to draw something for you," Prabuddh said and started looking around. "There, let us go there," he said pointing to a heap of sand across the road, and started walking towards it.

Viklav followed. Prabuddh picked up a stick in his hand. He rearranged part of the sand heap so that it formed a plateau, and started drawing on it with the stick. As he drew, he said, "Culture creation is a tough job, Viklav. It needs one to be very attentive constantly, and look at all angles of a particular thing. It is time consuming, but the results are worth the effort." He was done with his drawing in a minute. He had drawn a graph. It appeared as below:

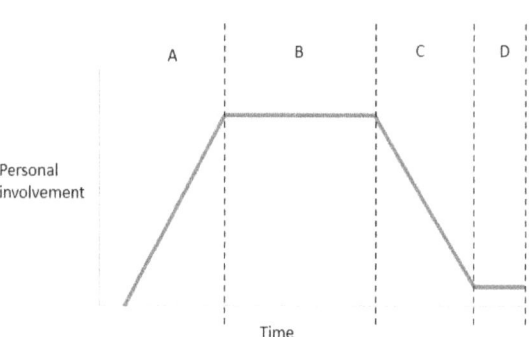

"This shows how culture is created. There are four steps from A to D. A is the start point. Here, from nothing in place you slowly start putting in few things through active intervention. The scope goes on increasing till you reach where you want to. Step B starts from this point. In this step, you maintain the focus on the cultural intervention and work on making the culture accepted and absorbed in the organization. Step C starts once you believe the culture has got absorbed. In this step, you slowly reduce the personal intervention and allow the process to work by itself. Once you have reached minimum intervention, step C ends."

"But why is the intervention required after this step –

why step D? Once the culture is created, should not it work on its own?"

"It should. But remember, everything created needs maintenance to keep it running smoothly. Step D shows the maintenance phase. We saw earlier that culture is a dynamic entity. It can change over time. It can change through action or through negligence. To ensure it does not change through negligence, you have to be watchful. At times after culture creation is completed, and you are in step D, old behaviour patterns can return. This needs quick action. The figure than becomes like this." Prabuddh made some changes to the figure he had drawn. Now it looked like this:

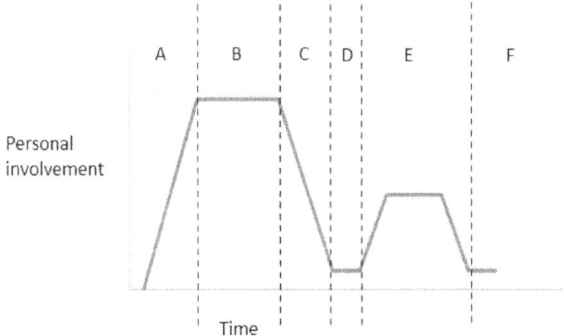

"Once a gap is noticed, it is time to increase intervention again, as shown in step E. But the extent of personal involvement in step E will be lesser than in steps A, B and C. Similarly, the time required to be spent on step E will also be lesser than the sum total of time spent on steps A, B and C. Repair is always easier than creation, provided it is done immediately after a defect is noted.

"The bigger point is that culture creation needs the two ingredients mentioned on the two axes of the graph – time on one side, and personal involvement, attention, and effort on the other. By investing in these two ingredients, you can reach a place from where culture will work on its own. Of course, you need to keep a watch through minimal observation to ensure that it continues to run the way you wish. In case you notice a deviation, quick corrective action can put it back in place. Another important point to note is how culture is introduced in step A. The personal intervention starts from zero and then moves to the maximum level over time in a slow manner. Culture has to always be introduced in a slow and consistent way, step by step, to ensure successful acceptance thereof."

Prabuddh kept the stick back from where he had picked it, and pointed his hand towards the road indicating they could resume their walk.

"What was the second point you wanted to talk about?" he asked.

"It is a question that has come from the Education Minister. One of our states, which is quite a distance from here has requested for an additional school. The state has two schools which cannot accommodate all students. So, those who cannot be admitted in the schools there, either have to come all the way to our capital city for education, or just give up on schooling. So, they want one more school. The Education Minister received the request, so he came to me for a decision. I of course, want to say 'yes', but in this case also, I thought I could take your advice."

"This can be a very good case study, Viklav. We can use this to strongly introduce culture. Thanks for bringing this to the discussion. So, let us put first things first. Why is your answer a 'yes'? "

"Education is one of the primary responsibilities of the administration. We have to ensure education for every child. There cannot be any compromise with this."

"Sure. I appreciate your firm and well thought response. So, has the Minister given you a complete proposal on this subject?"

"Umm….no."

"Would you not like to get all the information, the plan, resources required, constraints, and everything else before deciding?"

"Yes, but I do not want to delay the decision on that count. What is important …. is important. We will find the resources required from wherever. We will overcome the constraints, if any. That cannot stop me from deciding on the school."

"While I understand your emotion, I do not agree with it. I am sure you will find the resources and overcome the constraints. But if the resources required and constraints anticipated are known beforehand, one can prepare better for the same. If you are prepared, efficiency will go up and costs will come down. Secondly, why do you want to be the person making the decision?"

"So, who else will it be?"

"Your Council of Ministers. Let the decision be theirs and final approval be yours. If the decision is yours, the accountability will automatically rest with you. The team will come to you for everything. Instead, let them decide. Then, the accountability will be theirs."

"But it is an education related matter. What will the other Ministers add in value to an area which is not their domain?"

"It is one organization, Viklav. Everything is related. Every Minister can play a role in a related area. Hence, the whole team has to look at it. It is incorrect that you make the decision. It is further incorrect that you make the decision without having all required information. It is completely incorrect that you make the decision without keeping the rest of the organization in loop."

"What if they take a lot of time?"

"Be patient."

"And if they do not act at all?"

"Be persistent. Give them deadlines."

"It does not work that way here."

"That is the challenge, Viklav. You have to make it work. Or else just give up this culture exercise."

Viklav noticed that Prabuddh, for the first time, was getting slightly angry. He chose to remain quiet.

"A very important thing here is that the Education Minister cannot come to you with a mere question. Because if he is doing so, he is doing the job of a messenger. He is just transferring the question from its source to you. Where is his value addition in the process? It is his job to fully understand the requirement, have it discussed within his team, with his peers, get convinced himself and then come to you with a full-fledged proposal. You should come into picture only at that point."

"I am not sure that all of this can happen in time. I do not like delay in such matters."

"The fact that you do not like delay is very good. But

then how can you like the inefficiency of your people? Viklav, I know that you are not happy with the way the team works. But the other side of the coin is that you are not challenging them enough. You are not giving them adequate opportunity to try. They may fail as they try, but let them keep attempting. Remember, that getting into action everywhere is not leadership, though it may help increasing speed. True leadership is constantly challenging people to grow, because if they grow, you will automatically grow. Growth may come at a slower pace, but it will be sustained. Viklav, think to yourself – are you behaving like a large tree that does not allow anything to grow under it?"

"I have given them opportunities, Prabuddh. Number of them."

"You may not have used the correct methods. You may not have been patient enough. Viklav, you have kids at home. As children grow, you have to teach them so many things. How to walk, how to sit, how to speak, how to eat with their own hands – there are so many things. Parents have to use several methods in the process – they have to explain how a particular task is to be performed, demonstrate by doing, appreciate, punish, convince, compare, and do everything else under the sky. Can you as a parent give up on your child because the child is not ready to walk for example? Can you decide that you will walk on the child's behalf all its life? You have to constantly keep trying; else you are not fit to be a parent. While working with kids, you have to work at their level, at their pace. Probably, while working with your team, you expect the team members to be at your level, and if they are not, you give up on them. Please do not do that. Go to their level and pull them up from there."

"Ok," Viklav gave up on his resistance, reluctantly. "What should I do then?"

"Tell the Minister to come with a complete proposal including a recommendation. Do not tell him what process he needs to follow to reach there. Rather ask him what he thinks is the right process to arrive at the expected end result. Let him come with a proposed process, you only correct it."

"Ok."

"Let us meet another time to understand the structure of culture."

P-P-C

Prabuddh was waiting for Viklav in the meeting room. Viklav had not been able to find time for the meeting last few days, but Prabuddh wanted to take up his next theory class quickly. Finally, Viklav agreed to give him some time in the evening. But he had not yet arrived in the room, though Prabuddh was waiting there for quite some time. An attendant had served him water and had also placed some blank sheets of paper and a pen on the table. Prabuddh was happy to see the papers and pen coming in without having been asked for.

Prabuddh used up the time to think on some of the projects he and his team had started working on in his Ashram. He had enjoyed alternating between his Ashram and being out helping organizations. While the Ashram work allowed him to create hypothesis, work on them, discuss with the team, teach and learn in the process; his 'site' jobs allowed him exposure to various environments, and different sets of problems. This gave him learning opportunities and new knowledge that he could go back and share with his team.

Prabuddh worked on management of organizations, but his objective was achieving spiritual growth. For him, spirituality meant being able to lead a blissful life. He believed that spirituality is not necessarily a personal concept. Humans are social animals, and hence a person and the society he lives in are inseparable. They affect each other, and it is difficult for a person to achieve spiritual progress if the society around him is spiritually backward. Society is made up of organizations; hence the 'lifestyle' of organizations was a subject he had chosen for in depth study. His mission of life was to assist organizations to manage and organize their work better. This would enable its members to achieve spiritual growth. The improvement in organizations would ultimately culminate into the whole society being spiritually progressed, and in turn would help every citizen to achieve growth as well. Some of his peers in the field of spirituality had not appreciated the idea. They believed spirituality is totally person-specific and cannot be linked to kingdoms or other institutions. But Prabuddh was very firm on his idea. He wanted to train up a bunch of students, who would then go across the world teaching organizations how to be blissful rather than stressful.

Finally, Viklav came in. "My apologies Prabuddh. Sorry to keep you waiting for a long time," he said.

"That is fine," said Prabuddh.

"I had almost walked half the distance from my office, when I had to go back and deal with something very urgent."

"No problems, Viklav. Let us begin with today's session. I am going to talk about the structure of culture. For doing this, I am going to use the human body to illustrate what I will say. The human body is a very 'cultured' institution. Nature has created it in a way that it runs in a specific, defined way. It does so many complex jobs, but in a very simple manner. It has self-correcting and self-defending mechanisms, which are so spontaneous, that you do not even realize their presence. It is a very scientifically structured mechanism.

"Now, I have a question for you. How can you describe the human body? When you talk about the human body, what exactly do you refer to?"

"Well, the body is made up of the brain, the heart, lungs, kidneys, etc. It is a group of organs."

"Correct. And what do the organs do?"

"Each organ has its own unique function. Like the stomach digests food. The ears 'hear' and the eyes 'see'."

"Absolutely. So, you can define the body in two ways – in terms of the physical constitution, which is the organs, and in terms of the functions they perform. Within the functions, I like to divide them into two – communication functions and other functions. The communication function has a unique importance, because it works alongside every other function. For example, while the digestive function secretes juices and absorbs nutrition, the function gets triggered only when the sensors in the body learn that there is food, which gets communicated to the appropriate organ. Hence, the communication function is uniquely important. The communication function in the body is made up of two systems – the nervous system and the endocrine system. The nervous system works like an instant messenger system transferring signals from sensory organs to the brain and from the brain to everywhere in the body. The endocrine system is a monitoring system that keeps a track of certain key metrics in the body and secretes chemicals to regulate them. The non-communication functions include the digestive, respiratory, circulatory, reproductive, sensory, structural, muscular, and other systems. So, the body can be looked at as a set of organs, a set of communication functions, or a set of non-communication functions. Very similar to this, culture is also made of three dimensions. Anything in an organization will always have these three dimensions, hence culture affects and is affected by all three of them. Like in the case of the body, the three dimensions of culture are inter-dependent. Now, based on the comparison to the human body, can you guess what the three dimensions of culture are?"

"Let me try," said Viklav, "in place of organs in case of the human body, we will have departments in case of culture?"

"We could. But the problem is that while an organ has a defined individual quality, a department may or may not have the same. A department is also a collection of people, and individual members of a department can have differing qualities. So, the better unit to use is that of an individual person. Since, the dimension refers to all individual persons in an organization in general, I call this dimension as 'People'."

"Ok. So, using the same logic and based on the dimensions for the human body that you had identified, the other two dimensions of culture will be communication systems and non-communication systems?"

"Yes. But I word them differently. The commonly used word for a system in an organization is 'Process'. So, the second dimension is 'Process'. I call the third dimension as 'Communication' without using the word 'system'"

It was drawing time again for Prabuddh. He quickly drew something on a sheet of paper, and handed it to Viklav. This was the diagram he had drawn:

CULTURE TRIANGLE

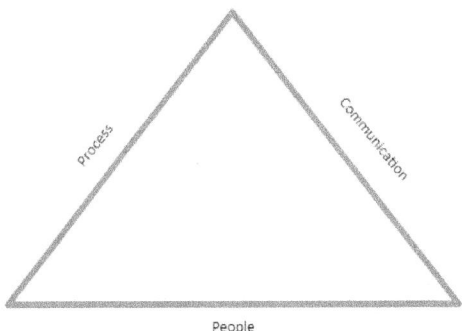

People

      "Since there are three dimensions to culture, organizational culture is best depicted by a culture 'triangle'. The three sides of the triangle represent the three dimensions. Anything and everything that happens in an organization will always fit in this triangle, and will have all the three dimensions to it. Say, for example, you are running a system of collecting taxes from the citizens. You will have to define how to decide the amount of tax to be collected from an individual. You will also have to define how the tax will be collected. This part of the transaction is covered under 'Process'. The decisions will have to be taken by someone. Someone will also have to implement the decisions. Who will do it? This will be covered under 'People'. To make the decisions, some information will be required. After the decision is made, it will have to be informed to people. This part will get covered under 'Communication'. The contents of the triangle can be viewed from any of the three sides. Depending on from which side you are looking inside the triangle, you will see the same contents but with a different perspective. If you see the triangle from the process side, culture will mean process to you. Ultimately, process will regulate how people work and how communication takes place. If you view the triangle from the people side, it will mean people. Whether process or communication, the action comes from people. The same would apply to the third dimension of communication. To have a successful organization, you need to have the right culture. To have the right culture, all three dimensions of the triangle will have to be strong. Weakness in any one dimension can render the other two ineffective, even if they are strong individually. For example, if an organization has the best quality people, but if the communication channels are weak, will the organization succeed? Similarly, if you have all the right processes, but the communication required to trigger a process does not happen in time, the process will not be effective. An organization has to ensure balanced growth of all three dimensions. This is the key to getting in the right culture. Lack of focus on any of the three can lead to failure."

"I have a question here;" Viklav spoke, "You said if communication is weak, even good people may not perform. But, good people can also put in the right communication practices......"

"True to some extent. See; let us say the head of a department sets on a task to improve communication. He can change how communication flows within his department. But, can he have the same influence on inter-departmental communication? No. Hence, what you say is right, but in a limited sense."

"In that case, the head of the organization can bring this change. Where is he in this triangle?"

"He is not. He is actually outside the triangle. He is expected to keep a watch on the triangle from all three sides, identify which dimensions have deficiencies, and work on them.

Pictorially, I depict the triangle as a part of a circle, the circle at Tier zero. The circle stands for culture. The difference between the circle and the triangle, depicted by the space occupied by the circle, but not occupied by the triangle, is the space where the leader operates."

Prabuddh quickly drew another figure on a sheet.

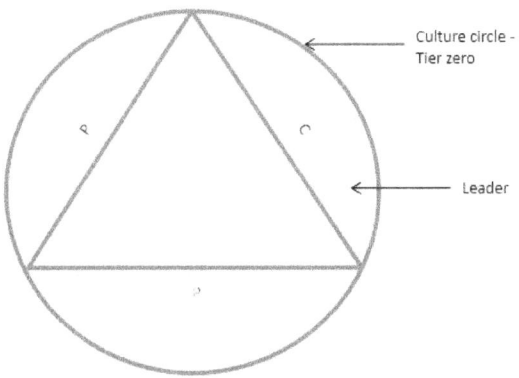

Culture circle - Tier zero

Leader

"It is important to note that the area occupied by the triangle is about half the area occupied by the circle. So, the other half is for the leader. This shows how important a role the leader plays in culture. We have spoken about this importance earlier. Now, let us focus on the three dimensions of culture – People, Process, and Communication. I call them P-P-C for short. There is nothing more to culture other than these three dimensions. If you want to change culture, you have to work on these three things. The three dimensions work in loops. Normally, a loop begins and ends with Communication. Hence, the loop is normally a C-P-P-C loop. For example, let us say I am feeling thirsty. I want to have water, so I call the attendant and request him for water. This is Communication (C). 'He' listens, so

People (P) comes into picture. He employs a Process (P) to get water, which he then places in front of me. This is also a visual communication (C) that the task is completed. So, one C-P-P-C loop is completed. The next one begins. I have received the communication that water is available. I drink water. 'I' is the People part. The way I drink water is the Process part. The attendant watching me drink water gets the communication that I have got what I wanted, so one more loop is over. If you are sitting next to me and have watched these two loops taking place here, you have actually witnessed a part of the culture of this place. The example I gave you explains culture with reference to one of the simplest transactions. There could be much more complex transactions. However, every transaction can be linked to one or several culture loops, and hence can be broken down into the lowest unit of P, P or C. When we say we have to change culture, it appears to be something huge. We do not know where to start from. But culture is finally an aggregation of culture loops. If you can break the whole subject into identifiable culture loops, and further into lowest units of P, P or C, it becomes very easy to maneuver them. For example, let us take up the matter of cooking food in this palace. This could be a complex transaction, with several people, several processes, and several communication points. But if you can get to the lowest unit of each of the three dimensions, it can be simplified for better control. Culture creation is a process of deciding on a new loop, or a change to an existing one, and seeing the loop through several repetitions, till the loop becomes spontaneous."

"This is interesting. Very interesting. I never thought of culture in such objective terms."

"It is objective. It is very scientific. That is why once you understand the science fully, applying it is not very difficult. Viklav, what we can attempt to do now is to apply this science to a particular transaction, and change the culture around it. It can be the simplest of all transactions. But as I said earlier, nothing works like demonstration. Let us demonstrate to ourselves how we can change things. We have so far understood how culture sits at tier zero in an organization. We discussed the triangle of culture, and the space for the leader. We looked at the P-P-C. We also understood the process of culture creation. It is good time now to actually try a change. We still have to look at what are the best traits to place in the culture triangle. The P-P-C ultimately works through these traits that the culture triangle houses. But that need not stop us. Can you think of some transaction that we can look at changing at this point in time?"

"Why not take the matter of wheat stock maintenance itself?"

"We are anyways working on that issue. But I do not think that is the one I am looking for. It needs to be something, the result of which should be seen quickly, and by a larger audience."

"I can think of something. One of the things I wanted to establish is discipline in terms of start time of our offices. Our administrative office officially starts at 8 am. But quite often I see that the people walk in at any time up to 8.30 am or sometimes up to 9 am. Can we look at doing something here?"

"That is a brilliant idea. Let us attempt changing this."

"Ok. I will make strict implementation of the time from tomorrow. Anyone late will be sent home for that day. I will have a notice displayed to that effect today itself."

"No Viklav, this is not the way. Why will you make the decisions? Why will you give instructions for implementation? You should pass this matter to your Council. Put the problem before them. Say that you need discipline. Let them decide whether 8 am is good, or the time should be changed to 8.30 am. Let them decide how to implement the discipline. Let them decide what will be the punishment. Let them decide from when to implement. Let them decide how to inform people. You only present the problem and ask for a solution by a specific time. Once they are ready with the entire process proposal, let them come to you. You give your approval after studying, and let it be implemented as per plan. Let the onus be theirs, Viklav."

Viklav smiled. He realized he had to curb his natural instincts of initiating everything and making decisions thereon.

"People are a very important part of culture building, Viklav. To strengthen culture, you should always involve them, not instruct them. But also take care that they should come to you with proposals, not ideas. If they come with a proposal, the accountability is theirs. If they come with an idea, it is yours."

"Yes Prabuddh, I get your point. I need to work on myself in this area."

"That is good. Now tell me what the latest on the wheat issue is."

"As we had planned in our last meeting, I did a follow up meeting with the Agriculture Minister. I asked him the questions you had raised. He told me that he had selected the monthly frequency for physical inspection, because a month's gap allows him to replenish the stock in time even if the reports during the month are incorrect. He has selected 5th of every month to do the inspection, and has also decided to keep a checklist of to-do items for better management of his tasks."

"That is excellent."

"When I asked him about the process employed for

creation of the report that comes from stores, he fumbled. He had not paid attention to that aspect. He went back and came again the next day with the process. Accordingly, one person who keeps records of stocks coming in and going out creates the report. Now, the Minister has added some more steps to the process. Accordingly, the report creator will do a visual check of the stock and corroborate with his data before creating the report, so that errors if any, can be corrected at the source. Next, another member of the team will check and validate the report before sending. He will also keep a register noting the errors if any that he observes in the weekly draft reports coming to him. This register will be used to discuss with the originator of the report for improvement in his performance and training on error-free work."

"I am really happy to know this, Viklav. The only care you have to take now is that the momentum you have created should not be diluted."

"Yes, of course. Probably, this is only step A of the culture creation process. I will give it the necessary attention and time. I have started using a checklist for my tasks with immediate effect. The review of the wheat inventory report on a monthly basis has been put into it."

"Do not forget now to also add the matter of office start time into your checklist."

"Yes Prabuddh, I will do that. There is also some update on the school proposal that I wanted to share. But I am running out of time now. I will speak to you on this matter in our next meeting."

The

Reinforcement

V iklav and Prabuddh were on their morning stroll. Viklav was meeting Prabuddh after a long gap. He had taken a tour of a nearby state in the kingdom, which had kept him away from the capital for a few days.

"So, what has been happening?" Prabuddh asked.

"Well, I have to tell you about the new policy as regards the start time for our offices. As suggested by you, I passed the question as regards the discipline part to the team. I gave them a couple of days to create a policy that will ensure discipline. It worked very well. The team came up with a complete policy. They decided to keep the start time at 8 am, but to change it during winter to 9 am. They have put in various checks to ensure that the time is followed strictly. The security team has been told to allow people to come in not more than fifteen minutes later than the start time. After fifteen minutes, no one will be allowed entry. The delay of fifteen minutes allowed for now will be reduced to five minutes over a period of two months. They also decided the time of implementation and the method of communication. All of this was planned and we actually implemented the new policy for the last three days. It has worked very well."

"Marvelous. Very happy to know this," Prabuddh said, "By following this method, you have ensured that the new process belongs to the Council. It is their process, not your process implemented by them. It is more likely to be successful this way."

"I was also impressed with the way they came out with matters I had never thought of, like having different start times for different seasons, or allowing a delay for now, and having a gradual reduction of the delay allowed."

"That is the fun of working in teams. A team has diverse approaches to the same problem, and if you do not take inputs from the team, and decide unilaterally, you do a disservice to yourself. The other advantage is that people feel empowered when you ask them to decide and deal with the problem."

"Yes. Thanks for this advice, Prabuddh. I have realized that though making decisions by me can speed up matters, involving people in decisions helps in making the decisions a real success. I need to learn the art of holding myself back from making decisions and get more decision-making done from the team, rather than pure implementation."

"Just a word of caution, Viklav. In this particular case, what has been done is good. But care is required to ensure that the work done continues. Please do not feel offended if you hear this statement from me repeatedly. Maintaining tempo is very important. If a system created fails, it is more damaging than not having a system at all. Regular monitoring will be required to ensure that the new system gets followed. I suggest this is something you should do yourself, by asking the right questions of the team members."

"Sure," Viklav agreed, "I will happily do that. I will have this put in my checklist right away."

Prabuddh smiled.

"One thing I have observed over last few weeks," Viklav continued saying, "My team members do not speak to each other very often. Or if they speak, it is very transaction specific. They hardly speak to each other when it comes to decisions or policy matters. The communication happens only when I direct them to do so. But whenever they do speak, they do brilliant work."

"I had guessed that this was the case right at the beginning," said Prabuddh, "But what do you think is the reason behind this?"

"I do not know."

"I think the reason is that there is no proper platform for such interactions to take place. Interactions happen only in your presence. There is no quality team interaction when you are not present. There may be no real need for such interaction in the current scheme of things. Decisions are usually made at your end, so what would the need for interaction be? You need to give your team more authority, more accountability, and then you will see that these interactions happen automatically. Send them back when they come with a question. Let them come with probable answers and recommendation. Let the recommendation be a studied one. This will necessitate interaction. Once you start involving the Council, once the Council members start talking to each other, the culture will automatically percolate downwards.

Even today, the Ministers would be copying your behaviour in their domains within their limited powers. They would not be allowing decisions at levels below theirs, and their teams would not be freely communicating as well."

"I agree. Prabuddh, there could also be something else that stops the members from engaging with each other. I think ego plays a role here. Going to a colleague asking for help or taking advice is like bending in front of the person."

"Yes, could be. When you, the King asks something of a team member, it is out of authority. When a team member asks something of another, it is like a favour. There can be two possible reasons behind this – one, that there is lack of trust among the team members, and two, that individuals have become more important than the objective. If objective is given all the importance, the personal egos will never come in picture. Better camaraderie within the team would ensure that these problems get resolved. Better camaraderie needs constant interaction which is free following and spontaneous. The people have to know each other better, they have to argue, agree, support, oppose, joke, share……. that is when they become a team. So, if this is not taking place, you will have to create situations which will ensure that they have to talk to each other."

"Yes. I think that is one area which will need a lot of attention from me."

"It definitely will. Remember, communication is one third of culture – it is one of the three dimensions. You cannot ignore it."

"Of course. I am already experiencing what can go wrong on communication in the case of the school proposal."

"So, where has it reached?"

"I had the matter discussed with our Education Minister. I told him that I expect him to study the matter and come back with a complete proposal. He was quite delighted with my response. But he had a concern to share. He said making a complete proposal will need a lot of time employed on it, and all that will go in vein if the proposal is rejected. His concern was genuine. But I followed what you had suggested to me sometime earlier – I did not give him a solution to the problem, rather asked him if he had a better way of dealing with this. He suggested that instead of a complete proposal, he will do a high level synopsis covering all matters, but in brief. If this synopsis is given an in-principle go ahead, he will come with a more detailed proposal."

"That is a great idea," Prabuddh exclaimed, "It appears to me that this person has excellent process skills, unfortunately he is not using his brains enough."

"I also liked the idea. So, I accepted his approach. Post that, I have followed up with him on a couple of occasions. He has taken up discussions with the relevant Ministers with regard to the proposal. One roadblock he has hit is with regard to the Finance Minister. The Finance Minister initially did not give time to the Education Minister. When he did, his quick response was that he will speak to me on the matter. The Education Minister, very hesitantly, told me about this, that his work has halted on this account."

"So, has the Finance Minister spoken to you about this matter?"

"Not yet."

"Have you asked him about it?"

"No. I was not sure how to do it. I did not want to project the issue as a complaint, because that can worsen the issue. I cannot have the Finance Minister feel hurt. He is the senior most of the team, at least fifteen years older than me, and has been there since my Father's time. He is very knowledgeable, manages his work very well. But there is a kind of a gap between him and the rest. Probably he feels it is below his level to coordinate with others. I cannot disrespect him either."

"Viklav, it is important to note one thing here. I completely appreciate your respect for knowledge and age. You are doing the right thing by giving him respect. However, in an organization, no one can be bigger than the purpose. No one, including the leader himself. If one person's behaviour is affecting your initiatives on culture, this cannot be allowed. You have to work on the behaviour of that person, irrespective of his age and status."

"But how do I do it?"

"Through communication. Talk to the Finance Minister. Tell him that you had given a job to the Education Minister and you believe that the Education Minister is waiting for an input from him. Ask him when that input can be given. Do it in a nice professional way. Do it in an 'enabling' manner rather than a 'questioning' manner. Let it be respectful, but let the message be delivered that the matter is important to you. Most likely, he will want to give his update or input to you. In which case, you tell him that the Education Minister will be presenting a consolidated synopsis, and it will be better if the input is given to him rather than to you."

"Ok. I will need to prepare myself for this discussion."

"You should. Normally, we do not give adequate attention to matters like this. But it is a very important matter. It is completely a P-P-C matter. You definitely need to prepare in order to approach it well."

"Sure, I will keep that in mind."

"Fine. Now, let us start looking at the constitution of the culture triangle. We have to look at what fits in well into that triangle to give us the desired culture. There can be numerous traits in an organization that can serve as a part of the right culture. I have chosen a few of them, which I give utmost importance to. That is what we are going to talk about from today. For today, I think we should take up one culture trait which is very relevant to our discussion of today, and that is the way an organization is 'integrated'. Integration is what makes an organization a single unit. It serves the purpose of diluting personal agendas, feelings, approaches, knowledge, skills, into making one unique form representing the organization which is much more than the sum total of the personal traits. We all know the story of how unity brings strength. A single stick can be broken easily, but a bunch of sticks is very difficult to break with bare hands. There are two important concepts here that add the strength – one, a bigger number, and two, being together. It is not enough to have ten sticks instead of one. They also have to be tied together, and tied properly. If they are tied properly, the individual identity of the sticks dissolves into forming a new entity – that of the bunch. It becomes a unit by itself, it gets a separate identity. It is a similar case with an organization. An organization is a group of people. The group becomes a team only if the strings tying the people together are strong and are properly placed. In this case, the strings are not physical. They are in the form of process and communication.

"Free flowing, quality communication is the primary reinforcement that makes an organization strong. Communication alone can build bonds amongst people. These bonds are essential to develop trust among people and to get their frequencies synchronized. Once this happens, they start understanding each other's language and enjoying each other's company. If this is not in place, when communication happens between two people, both are busy in several other things apart from what is being communicated - they are thinking about each other's statuses, motives, likes, dislikes, approaches, and so on. The result is that the efficiency of communication is much lesser. Additionally, the communication is directed partly towards each other's relative standing, rather than a common objective. The communication quickly moves in the direction of proving who is right or wrong, who has more experience, who demonstrates more intelligence, etc. If the bond is established and a feeling of trust is present, these things go straight out of the window. The common objective is what takes priority. Scoring points over each other is not on the table. Complaints get converted to suggestions. Bond-building plays a significant role in integrating the organization.

"The second important part in integration is that of a proper process of communication. It is important that once a piece of information has entered an organization through a member, that information needs to get filtered, sorted, summarized and passed to every point of the organization according to relevance. Look at the human body. When eyes see a thing, can the hands claim that they did not know about it? Never. Can the eyes decide, consciously or sub-consciously to hide a piece of information? Never. But in an organization, this can happen. People in custody of information may not share it with others. Even if they want to share, they may not know the right platform to share. The processes of communication play an important part here. It is the duty of the leader to ensure that the bonds between the team members get created and become stronger by the day. It is the duty of the leader to ensure proper platforms are established for sharing of information. This duty is fulfilled not necessarily by active intervention. It is rather done by creating the right environment and nudging people towards creating the right platforms.

"The few examples of issues we have looked at tell us that lack of integration is one of the biggest weaknesses in your organization. The team structure is very weak and a large part of the organization communicates with one another through you or on your trigger. This is what creates dependence on you. You, through your individual brilliance, and hard work, face that dependence. If you need to minimize the dependence, you have to put extra effort towards creating inter-person bonds and the right processes for communication."

"Prabuddh, I completely understand what you are saying. However, is the personal bond between two people not a personal matter itself? How can a third person work on this?"

"It is possible for a leader to work on building bonds between team members. In fact, it is the leader's duty to do so for his own interest. It needs a bit of tact. Getting these bonds strengthened plays a very important role in success of an organization. Hence, it needs to be given the required attention and due care. First, it is important to keep your eyes and ears open to what kind of relationship exists between people. You have to constantly watch how they interact. This will tell you which pair of people does not have a good rapport. It will also tell you if there is a person or persons who have problems with almost every other person. These relations and these people have to be put on the watch list. You can adopt different methods to get this sorted. First, it is best to have a hard and honest talk to the concerned person. Whatever is identified as important by you, your team needs to know that it is important to you. Second, it is necessary to create as many opportunities as possible for the concerned people to be together with a purpose. Create situations for them to interact and coordinate. When they expect you to serve as a bridge between them, send them back. If an inter-departmental question is asked of you, ask the person if the question has been asked of the concerned department. Some people will fall in line quickly. Some will not. You will have to keep talking to them."

"I get your point. This is another eye-opener. I would never have imagined that it important for me to work on building bonds between my team members."

"It is very important. Integrating an organization improves its efficiency multiple times. The quality of relations between individual members of the team and between the team as a whole, and the quality of platforms for sharing information provides the **reinforcement** that makes an organization strong. Working on reinforcing the structure of the organization is an important part of a leader's job. Leadership is generally understood as leading from the front. This is incorrect. Leadership is actually leading from behind, and coming to the front only when the situation demands. Strengthening the **reinforcement** is one area where the leader works from behind."

They had reached back at the palace gates.

"Thank you Prabuddh. I will see you next week."

"Just a point to note. Your Agriculture Minister suggested doing a synopsis for your consideration before undertaking further study. Consider if this can be made a standard process for any important proposal that comes up."

"Sure."

More of Less; and Good Mistakes

"We are going to discuss some important concepts today – some important parts of the right culture. We discussed how important it is to have an integrated organization last week. Today, we are going to talk about two other traits – being 'Focused', and 'Learning'." Prabuddh made his opening statement. Viklav and he were sitting in the guest house garden. Viklav got a bit delayed and missed joining the morning walk with Prabuddh, though he wanted to. Instead, he joined over breakfast. Prabuddh emptied a glass of tender coconut water and picked up a sheet of paper. He started drawing.

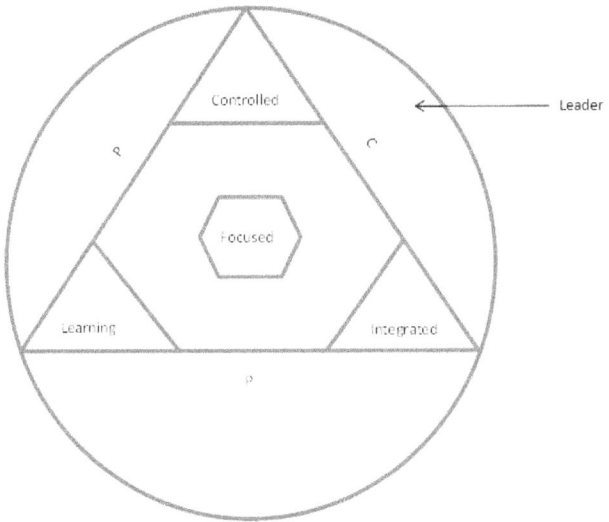

The artwork was partly familiar to Viklav. He recognized the culture circle, and the culture triangle with the three dimensions. But there was new stuff added inside the triangle.

"I believe there are ten primary traits an organization needs to have as a part of developing the right culture. I divide these ten traits into three groups. The first group consists of only one trait. I call this group the 'Centre'. The second group consists of three traits. I call it the 'Corner'. The third group consists of the balance six traits. I call it the 'Mid-centre'.

"The only trait in the group 'Centre' is 'Focus'. Focus has a unique importance in how we manage ourselves and our organizations. Hence, it sits in the group 'Centre' which is naturally, right at the centre of the culture triangle. The 'Corner' group consists of 'Learning', 'Integration', and 'Control'. These three together lay down a strong foundation for the right culture. They are important in their own way. As the name 'Corner' indicates, they sit in the three corners of the triangle. The other six traits sit in the space between the corners and the centre. We will delve into them at a later stage.

"It is important to note that all ten traits affect each other. They are inter-related, just like the three dimensions of culture are. You may find areas of overlap. We discussed the other day how an organization needs to be integrated. Similarly, the whole concept of culture is an integrated concept. We will study the individual parts of culture one by one. But ultimately, you have to look at the whole. Individual parts, in isolation, may mean nothing.

"Last week, we touched upon how it is important to have an integrated organization. We spoke of two important parts – one, having strong bonds amongst the team, and two, having proper platforms for communication."

"I wanted to share something here. I have been thinking over the creation of platforms. My Foreign Affairs Minister makes a report to me every time he takes up a foreign journey. He shares with me whatever new he has learnt which is of relevance. I realized that he could do the same thing with the entire Council. I have instructed him accordingly. He will now have a de-brief session with the Council after every journey. As I did this, I went one step further. I have now suggested the Council to have a meeting of their own, without me, at a regular frequency. Any new information that has come up has to be shared within that meeting. I have asked the Council itself to decide on the frequency, method, location, and so on. But my instruction is that when the matters come up at my meeting with the Council, I will expect a completely rounded input on any matter. It cannot be plain information coming to me. It will need to be a description of the matter together with the Council's recommended action thereon, or if the action is already taken then just information on the same for my validation. I believe this will save a lot of time. Normally whenever a topic gets discussed at my meeting, most of the Ministers have heard it for the first time, and every Minister uses that platform to share his views. If this process can be completed at their meeting, my meeting can only focus on the core issues."

"Yes. Viklav, I am really happy. You have understood the crux of the matter. Now, once the process has been put in, you will need to work to make it successful. If a topic does come up in your meeting with the Council, or in a one-to-one, you will need to send it back for the appropriate platform to process and then come to you."

"I will do that. The part B of the culture setting."

"Yes," Prabuddh said. He felt proud of the way his disciple has picked up the concepts. "Let us talk of focus now. This is a critically important principle. What does focus stand for in your opinion?"

"Well, focus is concentrating one's attention on a specific task."

"That is right. But there is more to it. See; let us say a tiger is on a hunt. He is chasing his prey in the jungle. His attention at that time is completely on killing the prey. There is nothing else in his mind at that time. This is focus. An organization also has a single goal in front of it, and it needs to focus all its attention on that goal. The focus in this case, may or may not be easily quantifiable, as was the case with the tiger's focus. Let us now talk about your kingdom. Can you define very briefly what the single goal is, that your kingdom needs to focus on?"

83

"We work to give the best to our people. So, you could say that the focus is welfare of the citizens."

"Good. That is a good goal to focus effort on. Organizational focus is a long-term, perennial, and an exhaustive way of defining what an organization wants. Having a clear focus is very important, and you have that clarity. The larger goal usually remains a statement in qualitative terms, like the one you spoke of. But the larger goal has to be converted to a quantitative statement to make it measurable, to have a commonly understood target to work towards, and to compare the performance against the target. This quantitative statement may have a short term or medium term applicability. For example, if you run a survey system with your citizens to measure welfare, and the welfare score is recorded as 6 out of 10, you could take a quantified target to move it to say, 6.5 or 7 over a specific time period.

"You defined the focus of your administration very clearly. The important thing now, is to understand how this focus relates to the organization, both at the micro and the macro levels. At the micro level, every transaction undertaken, every decision made, every instruction given, every communication made, by every person at every level, has to be done with the focus in mind. It happens that when we are in transaction mode, we may forget the larger focus, and get carried away by other short term objectives which may not be synchronized with the larger goal. This should not be allowed. Just to illustrate, if you have a senior resource with excellent caliber, but his behaviour is negatively affecting the welfare of people, your action regarding the matter has to give primary importance to the welfare and not his seniority or capability."

"Prabuddh, I have a problem I have to share with you at

this stage."

"Ok. Go on."

"My wife's nephew works in our administration. I had promised his parents that I will take good care of him. I have placed him in the Agriculture department. Unfortunately, his performance has not been up to the mark. I have reports that he is irregular at work, and our Agriculture Minister feels threatened because of his presence. I would frankly like to have him out of the organization, but then my commitment to his parents and my wife will be at risk."

"I have answered your question even before you asked it. It is the focus that has to take priority over a person or your commitment. If his presence is going to affect the performance of the team and culture of the place, which in turn can lead to diluting the focus on welfare of the people, he does not deserve to be here."

"But how do I face my family?"

"I did not mean you take him off immediately. But you can talk to him and his parents. Tell them that his performance and behaviour will have to improve. Give him an opportunity and some time for change. But let it be clear that if the change is not seen, he will need to quit. That will be fair to them, you, and the organization as well. Ultimately, the focus is important than anything else."

"Ok. I will follow your suggested route."

"Fine. So, the first thing we saw is that the smallest of every action has to be in line with the focus. The second thing is that the larger plans and projects undertaken have to be viewed from the perspective of resource availability. Let us take the example of the school project you are reviewing. Will establishing a new school improve the welfare of your people? Yes, it will. So, the first box is ticked. However, if the school project has to be successfully implemented, it will need sufficient resource. It will need money, material, labour, management time, and even your personal attention. At the micro level, this may look very simple. But at the macro level, you will have to aggregate all such plans and projects to check if you have enough resource availability to successfully implement all those projects. If you start say five projects at the same time, it is probable that one of them will get stuck halfway through because of lack of funds. If it gets stuck, it could mean say fifty percent of the project cost will get sunk in, in an unproductive way. Another project may not get desired attention from management in terms of reviews and control, so the cost may escalate say by twenty percent or the project may get delayed by say three months. The situation could very well lead to having five brilliant projects, but all being inefficiently executed. All five may be in line with the high level focus at the micro level. However, while analyzing at the macro level, you will need to check whether by doing all five together, will the welfare of people be truly achieved. By over committing resource, all the projects which were in the interest of people welfare at the plan stage, may result being against it at the delivery stage. A better alternative could be to select and implement only those many projects out of the five being considered, as the available resources may justify for efficient implementation.

"Thus, being focused means checking that a transaction on hand will contribute to the overall goal, checking that there is sufficient resource available to allot to it, and having the discipline and courage to keep out matters which do not fit in these two checks. As a part of our work life, we come across several ideas which appear interesting. It is important to say 'no' to them if they do not qualify under both the checks."

"But then resource limits cannot stop every project. You can also work on making resources available when needed, even if they are not today."

"Yes. But in that case you need to have a clear plan which will define how the resources will be made available and in what timeline. You can then keep working on attempting to raise the resource. But if this does not happen within the timeline, the project should be scrapped. It is also important to not to invest any type of resource in the project until availability of all types of resources is ensured. Committing to projects without having adequate resource backup makes the organization unstable. This instability is manageable for some time, but is very dangerous if the uncertainty prevails for a long time.

"There is another angle to focus. Once you have decided that a particular project is in line with the overall focus at the micro level, and also has sufficient resource availability to support it at the macro level, the next important part is how you maintain consistent focus on that project. Several times it happens that a project, which is brilliant at the plan stage, loses steam over time because there is lack of adequate attention being consistently applied to it. There has to be a way of tracking and reviewing projects at a regular frequency, so that they always remain on the radar and are given adequate importance. There is a concept called 'Tempo'. Tempo means the pace at which an activity moves. Running an activity at a constant speed always takes less energy than when the activity passes through a ramp-up or a ramp-down phase. It is simply the law of inertia in action. Once an activity has picked up pace, it is important to maintain that tempo through regular reviews. If this does not happen, the energy spent earlier to create pace is lost. A new effort is required to bring it back to pace, and if the start-stops happen far too often, the project can get delayed or lose relevance. If a task which has passed through the micro and macro tests vis-a-vis the overall focus does not get consistent attention, ultimately the organizational focus gets defeated.

"This concept can very well be applied even to routine tasks. Multi-tasking is completely against focus, if it means doing several things at the same time. If a meeting is discussing a particular topic, and a member of the meeting raises an issue not directly connected to that topic, the tempo of that meeting is lost. That issue could be important, but the issue can easily be noted and taken up for discussion as soon as the topic under discussion is done with. Diverting discussions mid-way is a very energy-inefficient way of dealing with things. For example, as we are discussing now, if you are thinking of some other matter you have to deal with, neither our discussion is done justice to, nor the matter you are thinking of. It is better to complete one task, and then move to another. So, overall focus is about synchronizing focus at the micro and macro levels, rationing efforts so that every initiative will get adequate focus, and maintaining of continuity of focus. Focus is the most fundamental component of culture.

"Focus means doing **more of less**, so that you can get more out of less. You have to limit the number of things you want to do – choose as less as possible, but give those things end to end attention – as much as possible. If you do **more of less**, less will give you more, meaning less resource can give more in return. Focus improves efficiency, and hence you can get a higher return per unit of resource invested. On the other hand, if there is no focus, as much resource you may have, it can end up giving you much less in return."

"'Doing more of less' – nice statement! I agree with you, Prabuddh, though I had never thought of focus the way you presented it to me. What I have seen in my organization is that whenever there is an emergency, we have been able to focus our effort in that direction, and hence have successfully dealt with it. Be it war, or a natural calamity, or anything similar, we have always been highly focused. But I realize now, that we have not been able to maintain similar levels of focus in normal circumstances."

"This is commonly observed," Prabuddh responded, "A natural calamity or a war provides an external stimulus which is responded to with focus. In general circumstances, there is no such external stimulus. The stimulus has to be internal – it has to come from within. The person or the organization has to feel a strong need to have focus. It has to be internalized."

"Hmm….. I think I have a significant part to play here," Viklav said, shaking his head, "I get excited with new things. I think this makes me lose focus on some of the things which we are already working on. Once it is out of the attention zone, all effort put in into it gets wasted. So, we end up working very hard, but not on the same job, not persistently, not focused."

Prabuddh patted on Viklav's back. "It happens," he said, "You have now realized the problem and acknowledged it – that is fifty percent of the solution."

There was a moment of silence.

"Are you ready for the next subject? Or do you prefer a break?" Prabuddh asked.

"No, we can continue," said Viklav. He was keen to know more. His mind was being opened to a new world. A world not made of new things, but new ways of looking at things. He was being told how seemingly unimportant things were actually very important. Viklav imagined himself sitting in the circle at tier zero, and looking at the contents of the culture triangle from all three sides. He smiled at himself.

"Let us now move to the next topic, that of 'Learning'. There has to be a special effort to make an organization a 'learning' one. This is a very logical principle. Let us take an actual example. See, all this while, when a decision was required to be made, your natural response was to make the decision yourself – be it a decision about a transaction, a process, or anything similar. Now, after several interactions between you and me, your natural response will be to have your team members to make decisions, or at least come up with recommendations, rather than just present problems. Is that correct?"

"Yes, absolutely," Viklav said with a nod of his head.

"I have introduced you to this concept. You have thought about it, digested the concept, and internalized it. You now have a new response to the same situation. You understand that there was a problem in the way you dealt with the situation earlier, or that there was a better way of dealing with it, hence you adopted the better way. So, effectively, you 'learnt'. Does a similar thing happen with your organization? When a problem occurs, everyone runs to correct it. Is there an effort put in to ensure that the problem does not repeat? If yes, then the organization is a 'learning' organization. Learning means identifying the cause of a failure, devising a solution to the cause, and internalizing the solution, so that the solution becomes normal course of action. We earlier discussed that with regard to the wheat shortage issue, a similar issue occurred four times in six years. This is a clear indication that the administration did not 'learn'. It worked very well on correcting the problem whenever it arose, but never on correcting the cause.

"Learning has four components – one, identifying the

root cause of the problem; two, creating a solution for the root cause; three, communicating and internalizing the solution; and four, tracking and dealing with repetitions of the problem, if any.

"When a problem occurs, the natural response to the problem is correcting the situation that has arisen. This in fact, is the right response. Whatever has gone wrong needs to be rectified. But equal importance has to be given to ensure that the problem does not repeat. To get to this position, the first requirement is to get to the cause of the problem. The cause of a problem has a layered structure, and it is important to travel from the most evident cause to the most fundamental one – the root cause. Every time an organization deals with a problem, a lot of energy is consumed. A crisis necessitates the organization to set everything else aside, get all its resources to deal with the problem, and to act very fast. This needs lot of energy due to which several other areas starve of the energy that they need. If an organization works on creating the right solution to the cause of the problem, energy is consumed only once and that too at a time of choice of the organization. Once implemented, the problem does not arise again, and hence this makes the organization much more energy-efficient.

"Learning needs to be practiced in synchronization with the 'integration' principle. Once a problem is faced, the root cause identification, solution creation, and implementation of the solution has to be handed over to a team consisting of all stake holders. This ensures that the solution is conceived by the team. The onus of its success is also with the team. When the solution is found by the person or the team that faces the problem, the chances of the solution succeeding are far better. While the solution to a problem is usually a transaction, the solution to the cause is always a process. The solution to the problem of wheat shortage was to buy expensive wheat and rationing supplies.

This was a transaction. The solution to the cause of wheat shortage was putting in right processes to ensure that the right data of inventory was available and the right actions were taken based on the data.

"For having a successful 'learning' organization, communication plays a very important role. It is important that every problem gets recorded; it is properly shared with the concerned people, so is the root cause and the solution. The record serves as a reference point to check the success of process implementation, as well as to check that the problems are not being repeated. Creating a record also creates a visual impact on the people, giving them confidence that the process of creating solutions is working. It also incentivizes them to proactively get into the 'learning' mode. The register of all problems faced and the four step process for dealing with the cause of the problem serve as important tools to create a 'learning' organization.

"If a problem repeats after having put in a corrective mechanism to the cause, it needs to be given special attention. A repetition of the problem could indicate that the root cause identification was not done properly, or that the design of the solution to the cause was incorrect, or that there was a failure in its implementation. Corrective action needs to be taken, where required.

"A point to note here is that success is not about making fewer mistakes. Any organization will always make mistakes. A successful organization is one that does not repeat its mistakes. **Mistakes** are **good** in a sense, since they tell you where and how you could go wrong, and hence prepare you to avoid those situations, provided you learn from the mistakes. If you do not learn from the mistakes, you can face the same problems over and over, depleting you of energy, and making it difficult to improve, or sometimes even sustain the existing performance level."

"Prabuddh, this concept of learning appears to be a very logical, and a natural concept. Every individual applies this concept in everyday life, in an automatic manner. But, the paradox is that it is not visible in my organization. Probably the reason is that we have not looked at it in a scientific manner. We never recorded the number of problems we faced, and how we dealt with them, and never kept this data in front of us."

"Yes, Viklav. This is a very important reason. Another probable reason is your personality. Probably, at a sub-conscious level, you have developed a liking for crises. You personally possess the energy, the creativity and the composure to deal with an emergency. Probably, dealing with a crisis gives you an immediate high of having been able to solve a problem, it gives you a satisfaction of how you intervened and got things right when no one else could deal with it. Viklav, human mind works in crazy ways, and many times our conscious selves are not even aware of this. It is important to note that a leader's success is demonstrated not by personal intervention, but by creation of a strong P-P-C culture making him as redundant as possible. The redundancy is only physical, because the right P-P-C structure ensures that the leader is virtually present everywhere in the organization."

"It is difficult to believe what you said about me.....that I may sub-consciously like crises. But let me reflect on it. I have never thought of the problem from this angle. If the root cause of the problem of not having a learning organization is with me, I will have to deal with it appropriately."

"Good. Well, I have covered both 'focus' and 'learning'.

We will take up 'control' in our next meeting, which will then cover all the centre and the corner group traits."

"Ok. Today's session was very enlightening. I need time to think over it."

"Viklav, I have to thank you for the kind of attention and response you have given to me for every thought that I have put forth."

"That is in my own interest."

"True, but I have challenged you on your personal traits so many times. You have been very open to consider each of those conversations. It is very difficult to do that."

"It is difficult. But the credit for that is also yours. The way you package and present the concepts, it is very difficult to outright reject them."

Prabuddh acknowledged the gratitude with a smile.

"There is some very good development on the school project front," Viklav said, "I had a discussion with the Finance Minister. His contention was that he was not going to have sufficient funds to finance the project this year. Hence, he wanted to pass the matter through me."

"So, what did you say?"

"I told him that in his capacity as the Finance Minister, his opinion will be very important. But the school project is also essential for its own reasons, and he should look at all possibilities and give the right input to the Education Minister. After our discussion, their meeting did take place. This, I am told, was followed by a meeting of the entire Council, initiated by the Education Minister. He has now submitted his synopsis about the project. The synopsis covers what is the exact need of education facilities in the concerned state, what kind of need may arise over the next ten years, and accordingly what size of school will be required. It spells out the estimate of expenditure on construction and maintenance. It deals with availability and remuneration of teachers, staying facilities for students from distant areas, arrangement for food and water, etc. Many important things have come out of the proposal.

"The first point is that while the need was only for a general secondary school, many departments have requested for specialized higher education in the same complex. Agriculture department has made a strong request for an Agriculture specialization, which could help in teaching the right skills and modern techniques of farming to the population in that region. Art and Religion departments have also come up with requests. As a consequence, the Education Minister has proposed a complete relook at the school policy, specifically in relation to higher education. The proposal is to consider having decentralized hubs for specific subjects in regions where they are most relevant, rather than centralizing all higher education in the capital city. I have approved a study on the proposal.

"The second point is that it has been decided that the selection of land for this project will have to be in line with the demand of the Agriculture department. It will need provision for having agricultural land adjacent to the school complex, and having the right topography and the right quality of soil.

"The third point is that the Finance Minister and the Education Minister, after considering the funds availability, have come up with an idea that we do the project implementation in stages. Even if we do the whole project at one go, we may not have sufficient quality teachers available immediately. So, they have proposed that the project be implemented over a three year period. The building will be constructed in a modular way, so that Phase 1 can be put to use as soon as it is constructed. In the next two years, the People department and the Education department will work closely on identifying graduates interested to take up teaching as a profession, and will provide them professional training on teaching, so that by the time the project begins full-fledged, the required number of teachers will be available locally."

"Wow. Your team has really put in good thoughts and effort."

"They have actually surprised me. I was not aware that we had this kind of intelligence with us."

"Intelligence is important, but I think it is not as much about intelligence as much as it is about working together. Working in teams is like a drug. It gives you a different level of satisfaction. You have made them to work together. You have also told them that their work will get importance. This has given them a different kind of push to come out with their best."

"I am very excited about this."

"But you also need to exercise care. The various points that have come up from this study have to be followed up. You have to shift your focus from telling people what to do, to indicating to them that the task that they have taken up is very important for the organization. This is done by showing that you are personally reviewing the progress of every idea."

"I will definitely do that. In fact, I have asked the team to come with a proposed update reporting process in connection with the school project for my review. I do not want to tell them on which matters they need to report on, at what frequency, who should make the report, etc. I rather want them to recommend what they think is right. Once I approve of the process, I will put it in my checklist for regular review."

"Excellent. This update is very heart-warming."

"Just a last thing before I leave. While the school project is an expense item for us, the Foreign Affairs Minister has come up with a revenue angle to it. He believes there is good scope to offer the Agriculture higher education as a service to nearby kingdoms, and there is opportunity to make some income which can part finance our costs. Besides, it can also help to strengthen relations with those kingdoms. I am really amazed of how one matter can be looked at from several angles."

"That is the beauty of team work. It can do wonders. Provided that the members of the team should have expertise and experience in diverse areas, they should carry a positive approach, and the intra-team relations should be excellent."

"This is just the beginning. I only hope that they continue doing the same," said Viklav, but quickly realized he could articulate the sentence better. "No, no. I should rather say I only hope that I continue to put in my effort to ensure that the right team spirit prevails in the organization, and continue giving them more authority, and challenging them further."

Prabuddh smiled indicating agreement.

Caring; &
Planning End
to End

"**G**ood morning Prabuddh," Viklav said as he got down from the royal chariot. He walked towards Prabuddh and joined him on his morning walk. Viklav had reached at the guest house late by fifteen minutes, by which time Prabuddh had started on his morning walk. So, to catch up with him, Viklav used the services of his chariot. Prabuddh waited for a moment, greeted him, and the two started to walk amidst sounds of the constant flow of river water and bird chirping.

"We had to talk about 'control', right?" Prabuddh was straight on the subject.

"Yes, Prabuddh. But prior to that I have some developments to share with you."

"Of course. Tell me."

"The first thing is about the school project. I had a full-fledged meeting with the Council and have cleared the budget in-principle as per the Council's recommendation. The team has submitted a review calendar with respect to all ideas and proposals which are part of the overall proposal. Accordingly, I have incorporated those reviews in my checklist. The complete proposal including land identification, detailed timelines and costing, will be submitted in a month's time. I am very happy with the progress here.

"I had a very open chat with my wife's nephew. I have explained to him that if there is no performance, I cannot assure him a position. I have also spoken to his parents as well as my wife. He seems to have taken it in the right spirit. I had my People Minister spend some time with him. As a part of the discussion, it came up that he does not like a routine job, but is more interested in project type work. The People Minister then spoke to the Education Minister, and they both feel that he may do a good job as the Project manager for the school project. The two of course know his relation with me, and quite possibly this may have influenced their decision. But I have accepted the proposal and have very transparently told my wife's nephew that he will be under watch. I have decided to give him a chance with a timeline of two months. I will be reviewing his performance on a weekly basis over this time along with the Education Minister and the People Minister."

"I think this is a fair decision, Viklav. The best thing I have liked here is that there is full transparency on the current status of the matter and the plan. The two Ministers, yourself and your relative are all exactly on the same page about where the matter stands. If, on a similar basis, the weekly review and resulting feedback is shared openly, what happens later will not be a surprise to anyone. The ride will become smooth without any bumps."

"Yes. A third update is about the new policy regards office start time. I have come to know that the Council has taken certain decisions after a review of how the policy has feared over its first week. On a weekly basis, they will be creating a report with names of people who entered office up to fifteen minutes late, and of those who came at the gates later than fifteen minutes from the start time and were sent back. The first week's report has been made, and the People Minister has been assigned the job of talking individually to each person figuring in that list. The personal attention given has had a surprising effect on their entry times. There is compliance by almost every person the Minister has spoken to, from the following day."

"That is natural," Prabuddh said, "Personal discussions have a very different impact. We get used to communicating to people at the mid and lower levels of hierarchy through notices pasted on walls, or announcements made in teams. The one-to-one chat is a very different thing. It is a means of telling the person that he or she is important for the organization, and that is why a senior team member is spending time with the person. Further, if the person agrees in the one-to-one meeting to change his behaviour, it becomes a personal commitment given by him to another person, not to a faceless organization. The chemistry is completely different. But all in all, this is a brilliant job. It is outstanding."

"Prabuddh, the important thing is that I had nothing to do with any of these new initiatives taken with regard to the office start time. I did not even push people to do anything like this. If I had to decide, I would not have done it in this manner. My method would have been much inferior." He paused. "My people are better than me. They can think of novel approaches, and can consider so many different possibilities." Viklav's voice choked. His emotions were getting better of him. He was sensing the pride a parent experiences seeing his child achieve something, as well as a feeling of joy over the quality of people his team had.

"Viklav, it is important to note a few things here. One, as we have discussed earlier, the strength of a team is always multiple times the strength of one person, provided the team is 'integrated'. Two, the effect you are experiencing, apart from integration, is also due to empowerment. The team now feels that they have decision making power. This feeling of having power is a great motivator. While these developments are good, there is a third ingredient that you must remember - the need to have a proper review system. While power improves motivation, review further enhances it. A proper review system tells people that their boss is going to look at how they have used their power, which also tells them that their job is important to the organization. Many times, leaders fail to give power to people, or when they give power, they give it without review. Both situations are equally bad. It is surprising, but both scenarios lead to stopping growth of the person. It Is a natural need of any person to have power, and to get positive and negative feedback for work done. Hence, it is important to delegate power, and regulate it. Ultimately, the responsibility of ensuring this happens in the organization rests with the......."

".......Leader," Viklav cut short Prabuddh's sentence, pointing to himself. They shared a good laugh.

"Viklav.... Since we discussed issues concerning dealing with people, I would like to take up now that culture trait from the mid-centre group which is relevant to this area and that is 'caring'."

"Ok."

"Care for citizens has always been an important matter for you. Similarly, for making the best use of people within an organization, the organization needs to first take good care of people within the organization. Being caring is one of the most important essentials for a successful organization. Finally, an organization is made of people, and it is important to take good care of people, so that they will take care of the work. What is important here is what you mean by 'care'. Care for me, is treating people like the way we treat a capital asset and giving adequate attention to their upkeep and maintenance. If we construct a building, or build a chariot, the value of that asset remains intact only if the asset is serviced and taken care of. People are often treated as expense rather than asset, because they are paid a salary and not an upfront cost. But this is incorrect. People should be treated as assets. Taking care of people is very important.

"Taking care of a building or a chariot primarily deals with the physical aspects. Taking care of people primarily means taking care of their minds. If the mind of a person is not in the correct mode, the performance of the person is not likely to be great. On the other hand, if the mind carries the right feelings, chances of the person being a good performer will be very high. Every person is unique and hence, the mind of every person works differently. So, it is very difficult to create a single method of dealing with everyone. However, caring for a person primarily covers five areas.

"The first area is what we already discussed when we spoke of 'integration'. People like to feel being part of something. They like to work in teams rather than being isolated. The interaction with people across departments and levels makes them feel nice. A leader's responsibility is to ensure that every person is 'accepted' by the organization, and gets opportunities to interact with several people.

"The second area is about giving importance to people. Every person in the organization should feel that he is contributing to the organization. Every person needs to be given adequate time to explain what importance the work of the person carries in the overall scheme of things. The person needs to be given adequate power. The person's opinions need to be heard. A senior has to ensure that he does frequent one-to-one meetings with every junior. The one-to-ones should focus not only on giving instructions and doing reviews, but also encourage the junior member to speak and give his opinion, share ideas, point out issues, etc. There should also be separate one-to-one meetings conducted not to discuss work, but to discuss the person himself – his personal matters, plans, family, goals, etc.

"The third area is having a clear definition of the role of every person and where he stands in the hierarchy in the organization. If there is ambiguity with regard to what exactly is the scope of work of a person, who does he report to, and who reports into him, it leads to confusion in the mind of the person. Establishing authority and accountability becomes difficult, hampering performance of the person as well as the organization. Hence, it is important that every person knows in very clear terms the boundaries within which he has to operate, and that there is going to be no one else operating in the same boundary.

"The fourth area is having the right appreciation and correction techniques. A good job done needs to be appreciated. A bad job done needs to be discussed openly. This should be done not with an objective of putting blame, but with an objective of ensuring acknowledgement of the error and devising methods so that the error is not repeated. Many times, a senior's response to a mistake made by a junior is either to overlook it, or to deal with it with an angry outburst and shouting. Neither of this works. It is important to point out mistakes, in a nice way, but also indicating how important the task done by the person is for the team, and hence it has to be done with all care.

"The fifth area is with respect to challenging people. If a person is doing the same job month after month, year after year, with the same methods, the growth of the person stops, and the person will lose interest at a point in time. A person needs to be constantly challenged. He needs to be given a change of job, a new responsibility, a new problem to deal with, after he has spent a reasonable period in a status quo situation. There should also be a plan drawn by person indicating what could be the growth opportunity for him over the foreseeable future. These five areas together are about caring for people."

"Prabuddh, I have already seen the positive outcome of integration of people, and giving power and importance to them. I have understood how important these areas are. I can also relate to defining roles of people clearly as a requisite. But the last two points you mentioned are novel to me. Somehow, I never associated caring for people with pointing out their mistakes, or giving them newer responsibilities."

"See, if you are not transparent with people as regards their failures, or if you do not present to them new challenges, you are denying them an opportunity to grow. If mistakes are not discussed, they will never improve. If they are not given new tasks, they will never develop. Helping people to improve and develop is caring for them. Discussing mistakes or giving new work may be perceived negatively in the short term, but ultimately it allows a person to reach his true potential, and keeps his intellect lively. If there is no improvement or growth, a person's mind starts becoming sick. His value deteriorates. His performance goes down."

"Understood. This culture trait – caring, where does it fit in the culture triangle? Is it in the blank space you had kept in the triangle when you drew it last time?"

"Yes. It is part of the 'mid-centre' group of traits. The hexagon at the centre of the triangle less the area occupied by 'focus', has six culture traits within it. 'Caring' is one of the most important among them. I took it up now since it was very relevant to our discussion."

"Ok. So now we take up the one 'Corner' group trait that we had to discuss – 'control'?"

"Yes. Let us talk about control now. Let us take a very simple and real time example to understand control."

"Real time?" Viklav asked with a smile, "Are you going to talk about our morning walk?"

"Precisely. Tell me, if I continue walking like this, without paying attention to the time, to the distance I have walked, or to my energy levels, what will be the outcome?"

"You may reach really far away from the palace."

"Correct. Another possibility is that at some point, I may get drained of energy and may collapse. I will call this situation as being out of control. Now, if I want to control this activity of walking, what should I do?"

"You could decide a time limit up to which you will walk in this direction. Post that time, you walk backwards."

"Right. I could also decide on a milestone. Once the milestone is reached, I go back. Normally, every day, I walk up to the coconut farm that you can see ahead. That is my milestone. So, deciding on the milestone is the first step. The next step is to keep a constant watch to check if the milestone has been achieved, or how far we are from the milestone. The third step is to take the action of turning back once the milestone is achieved. This is how control is established. In organizational parlance, the first step is having a plan. There has to be a specific target and a plan to achieve that target. The second step is having regular reviews. The plan has to be converted to a checklist and every item in the checklist allotted a particular frequency of review. A proper review system has to be put in place so that reviews happen at a specific frequency, and necessary data is available for the review. The reviews have to be done as per the system, and the next action has to be initiated based on the result of the review. If the check listed items are happening as planned, you just follow the next sequential action. If there is a deviation, a new action may be required, which could also involve a change in the plan itself. Say for example, as I am walking, it starts raining heavily. This information has to be picked and submitted to the review system. Fortunately, my sensory organs and brain are on a constant vigil. So, the eyes, ears and skin will report that there is rain and the brain will decide that it is not appropriate to continue the work as planned earlier. It may decide on other possible actions like taking shelter under a tree, or a nearby house, or just running back to the guest house towards safety. This is the simplest way of explaining control."

"What if you want to enjoy getting wet in the rain?"

Prabuddh laughed. "This would also be fine provided it is a consciously decided action," he said. "But if you keep walking in the rain because you have not realized it is raining, then obviously it is not good."

"This is what happens in our organization. We are not a controlled organization. Definitely not," Viklav exclaimed.

They had now reached the coconut farm. Both of them slowed down and eventually stopped. They looked at each other and started walking back towards the palace.

"I know that the organization lacks control," said Prabuddh. "Now, think about it. We discussed a three-step process to control. Which step it is in your opinion, where the organization falters?"

"I think it is the review. The reviews never happen on time. People are never on top of the situation. You will ask them, and they will check and come back, and then the action gets initiated. If you do not ask, no one checks. I think we are fine on the other two steps – Planning and action. Our planning is decent and quite detailed. In fact, at the plan stage, every proposal looks great. But it never lives up to the potential. Our actions are also swift. As I had shared earlier, whenever a problem arose, we were into action immediately. The issue has been getting to know of the problem in time, and we are poor at it."

"Viklav, I understand the weakness in the review step. However, if I say that the failure is actually of the plan step rather than the review step?"

"Why would you say that?"

"Because a review also needs to be planned. Planning does not end at creating sequential steps required to achieve the target. The sequential steps have to be converted to a checklist, and the review calendar for the same also needs to be defined. The plan should also specify who will be collecting the information and at what frequency, who it will be shared with and how, and who will look at it. Having this clarity upfront is key. It helps in setting the right expectations. If you have a meeting to discuss and decide on something, the meeting cannot end at the decision making. It also has to provide for who and when will implement the decision, who will check how it is performing, and who and when will review this information. The **planning** has to be **end to end**.

"Another important point is to identify risks in the plan. A plan is for the future, and the future may not behave the way we want it to. Hence, while making a plan, we have to identify which areas of the plan are critical, and hence need to be monitored carefully. The plan should, where possible also provide for alternative routes to be taken if the original plan with respect to the critical area fails."

"But then this will take a lot of time at the plan stage. We are not used to working like this."

"That is exactly the problem. There is no point in getting excited about something and commencing implementation before having done an **end to end planning** including planning for risks and planning the review."

"Somehow, I still cannot understand the need to do this. Let the review process be decided once the matter comes in the review pipeline."

"This can work only in specific situations, either when the scale is small, or when the communication system is highly efficient. Neither is true of your organization. Planning for review helps in making the plan stronger, and the review timely. Let me give you an example of how this works. Let us talk about your communication with your son. Do you schedule a specific time with him on a daily basis when he has to report to you all that he did during the day? Not probable. No one does it. Communication between you and your son happens naturally whenever it is required. No planning is required. That is because your family is relatively small and the quality of communication within is good. Now, if I add some complexity to this situation...... let us imagine that your son decides to get admitted for education into a distant university, say for five years. He will not be back till he completes five years. In this case, how will you manage communication with him during the period?"

"Umm..... I may tell him to write letters to us intimating the developments at his side."

"How frequently?"

"Once a month should be good. We will need to be informed of his wellbeing and how he is doing at his studies. A monthly frequency should serve that purpose."

"So, in short you would have to make a plan for review upfront, before he left for the university. The expectation would be set clearly right there. This became necessary because there was complexity added to the situation – complexity of your son being miles away from you and not having open communication channels all the while. Similarly, when you have an organization of the size of your administration, the scale is too big to leave the review plans for later. The scale makes the situation complex. With hundreds of tasks to manage, unless a review plan is in place, some of the items can get lost. Hence, it is crucial to create a plan for review, and incorporate it into a checklist. More importantly, every person needs to have a checklist and the list needs to be checked!"

"Ok. So, what you are saying is that working in an organization has a higher level of complexity because the number of people involved and the number of tasks to manage is much higher compared to a smaller unit, say family. The complexity demands that the plan cover as much as possible."

"Yes," said Prabuddh, "If the plan is as detailed as possible, and also provides for how the reviews will be done, it is always easier to exercise control. The plan should give special importance to the critical areas through more stringent reviews. It should also provide for a plan B and a plan C to be employed if the plan A in such area fails. To control effectively, we need to know what to compare the performance against, which is given by the plan steps, and we need to do the comparison in a timely manner, which is ensured through the review mechanism. Of course, based on the review, the actions required have to be taken to get the performance in line with the plan, if it has deviated from it. Communication plays a very important role in exercising control. To do a review, we need to have a report on the actual performance, which is a form of communication. Similarly, the outcome of review may need action from several people, again requiring communication with all concerned. Successful control calls for an 'integrated' organization."

"So, as I see it, the checklist is the primary tool in control, and the checklist has to be created or updated as soon as the plan is ready. Or probably, creating the checklist has to be a part of the plan."

"Yes. Viklav, a while back you looked unsure of having the review mechanism defined in the plan. Probably as a theoretical concept, you looked at it for the first time. But we have discussed this concept in practical parlance earlier, and may be you have not realized, but you have already started practicing it."

"We discussed, and I have implemented? When?"

"Yes. At least on two occasions earlier, when you gave a positive update on certain things, I had reminded you that you need to ensure that momentum created on any activity needs to be maintained through proper and timely reviews. Now recollect what you said at the beginning of today's meeting. You informed that your team has given a review calendar with respect to the school project and you have incorporated it in your checklist. You also said with reference to your wife's nephew, that you will have a weekly review for the next two months. So, you have actually understood the importance of what I am saying very well."

"Oh….." Viklav laughed out, "Yes, and why did I not realize this when I was not agreeing with you?"

"Could be because you implemented what I said with reference to only the specific transaction which was being discussed. Now, we have looked at the concept from a macro perspective, something which has to be an integral part of a control system, wherein the matter to be controlled could be anything. From this perspective, the theory may have sounded unfamiliar to you."

"It is crazy. But now I understand and accept as a concept what I have already started practicing. I also understand that what I have started practicing at my level; I need to make it an organizational habit. *End to end planning* is the key to exercising control. Every plan should also include a review calendar. The reviews should give importance to the critical areas of the plan. Critical areas should also be covered up with backup plans for use in case the original plan fails. The reviews planned have to be done religiously. The checklist is the primary tool for doing this. Timely and good quality reporting is essential for this review. The reviews have to translate to action points in the organization. Communication plays a key role both in getting the reports, and creating and implementing actions."

"Excellent. Thanks for summarizing so well."

"Prabuddh, I must say this ...... the way you present things, it is very difficult not to understand them. Concepts which appear complex become very easy and completely obvious when they come from you."

"Thank you."

"So, at the concept level, we have to now deal with the other culture traits which are important?"

"Yes. We covered 'caring' from the mid-centre group and 'control' from the 'corner' group today. Let us do the other traits from the 'mid-centre' group next time."

"I have taken up creating a summary of all that we have discussed so far. I will share it with you once done."

"That will be lovely."

Mid-centre

V iklav and Prabuddh were sitting in the conference room. It was late evening. Viklav appeared a bit stressed, but Prabuddh was calm as usual. The meeting was decided very late.

"Prabuddh, I am very sorry for the news that has come in. One of your disciples is apparently very sick."

"Yes. His name is 'Satatv'. He is a brilliant boy. I have lot of expectations from him. I got the message today morning about him being unwell. Looks like it is something serious. I need to go back. Your Foreign Affairs Minister told me a while ago that they are arranging a ship tomorrow morning."

"Yes. I hope he will be all right."

"Me too."

"It is sad that you have to leave abruptly. I had so much more to learn from you."

"I am a bit worried about Satatv. However, I do not really feel that we are leaving our culture project halfway through. To tell you frankly, I was anyways thinking of concluding our work shortly."

Viklav did not say anything but his face had the question 'why?' written on it.

"If you analyze where we started from and where we have reached, we have covered a lot of ground. But more important to me is not how much we have walked, but how we have done it. I do not know whether you have realized it, but the way you think has substantially changed over last few weeks. Whatever small successes you have seen over this period have occurred only because of this change. It is not that you have blindly followed whatever I said. Rather, you have thought over the concept that I have shared, and have absorbed it. Once it is absorbed, the action has come from you as an action that you have decided, not as an action that I have asked you to do. This gives me a lot of confidence and tells me that the process we have begun will continue with or without me. My job was to prepare the soil in your mind, and sow the right seeds in it. You have more than reciprocated by taking adequate care of those seeds and the plants that have grown from the seeds. I am not really worried now. I was thinking of winding up this project over next couple of weeks. In line with what you have done to me, your team also has done exactly the same to you. I am sure that this process will continue till it reaches the last man in your administration team. My role was only to give you a conceptual understanding of the subject. Once the concepts are clear, they have universal application."

"But I was not ready for it so soon."

"I can understand. But you must note that though I have been here for about two months, we have actually met only seven or eight times. The objective was that you get adequate time by yourself to think on the concept, absorb it, practice it, and

114

provide feedback to me, before we take up another subject. This has worked very well. If we would have met every day, it would not have had the same rate of success. But the most important thing is the seriousness with which you dealt with this project. We met only seven or eight times, but you have been on this subject every day in these two months. You might have achieved less, but as we discussed earlier, the foundation has been created. That is the key."

"I agree, Prabuddh."

"Anyways, thanks for finding time from your schedule for this unplanned meeting. I want to discuss the balance mid-centre traits before I leave. I hope you have the time for it."

"Of course. I have kept everything aside for today's meeting. I cannot afford to lose these precious moments with you."

"We will discuss five culture traits from the mid-centre group today. They are – discipline, simplicity, flexibility, humility, and being analytical.

"The first trait I am going to talk about is discipline. Discipline is something that affects every other trait in the culture triangle. To achieve focus, you need to be disciplined. To achieve control, you need discipline of reviews. Similarly, whether its integration, caring, learning… everything needs discipline. You and your administration have taken some steps as regards discipline, which is good. Creating discipline around start time for your offices is a project you have already implemented. You have also started using the checklist as a tool for conducting reviews. However, one thing that I have not seen a lot of improvement on is discipline as regards time management. You have frequently ended up reaching late to our meetings. It tells me that something is not quite right in this area. You cannot get late so many times."

"The delay happens due to many reasons, Prabuddh. Sometimes, an earlier meeting takes more time than was planned, so the next meeting gets delayed. Sometimes, an unexpected item comes up for discussion; hence I reach late to meetings. There is always a reason."

"I agree. But it gives a very wrong signal to the organization. Remember, demonstration is the best way of creating culture. By doing what you are doing, your message to the organization is that being late for meetings is acceptable."

"So what can I do about it?"

"You have to find the root cause. Find why this happens. If one meeting takes more time than planned, and this affects the schedule of the next meeting, then there is something wrong in the way the meetings are planned. Probably you are giving less time than adequate for the meetings at the scheduling stage."

"I do not think so. Many a times, our meetings work in a way that as much time you allot to them, we always run short of time eventually."

"In that case, there is something wrong in the conduct of meetings."

"Yes. Most of the times, our meetings focus on the problem rather than the solution. We talk and talk, and keep on talking. But no one says what should be done or what can be done."

"This is something you must stop immediately. Take care that when you schedule a meeting, it is done well in advance, so that there is sufficient time given to prepare to the

116

people. The second thing is that what is expected in the meeting from an attendee should be made very clear to him upfront."

"I always do that. But it does not work."

"So if during the meeting you find that it is not being conducted as you want it to be, close the meeting and send the people back. Ask the people what next date they can come prepared, so you could schedule the next meeting at that time."

"But I cannot do this for every important matter. Everything will get delayed."

"You will not need to. Do this a few times. The message will be loud and clear. The quality of meetings will automatically improve. Show to people that you are serious about time and that you value time – your time as well as their time. Viklav, a meeting is a great opportunity for culture setting. It allows you to give a culture message to many people at the same time. As of now, you are giving incorrect cultural messages through your meetings. Getting late to a meeting has become a norm. Probably, having disorganized meetings – meetings at short notice, meetings without agenda, agenda without preparation, no sequence being followed, - all of this may have become a norm. Overrun of the time resource may have become a norm. This has to change. This will be a great step towards bringing discipline."

"Ok. I will attempt improving on this."

"Good. Another thing to remember is that you should have in a meeting only those many people as can actually contribute in the meeting. This is one area that needs a lot of care. Sometimes, for sake of speed, we tend to get many people to a meeting, which can at time affect the efficiency of the meeting. Look at the way the two of us have interacted. The efficiency of our meetings has been very high. But imagine that my meetings, instead of being with you alone, were with the whole Council of Ministers. In that case, could we have achieved that kind of efficiency? The way we worked is that you picked up the understanding of the subject from me and then passed the message to your Council at an appropriate time and place. Too many people in a meeting can mean more confusion, weakening of hierarchy, and of course, wastage of time. So, this is where discipline plays a role.

"Let us now move to the next trait, that is simplicity. Everything that we do needs to be as simple as possible. If the plan is simple, people understand it better, it is easy to remember, and hence, people like it more. Its implementation is likely to be successful to a greater degree as compared to a plan which is complex."

"This is very logical. But why will we do things in a complex way? We will naturally like to keep things simple."

"We intend to, but we may not actually end up doing things that way. The reason is that when we look at a particular transaction, we may feel the need to add a little bit of complexity to achieve a short term goal. At that point, with the goal in front of us, we may not even realize that we are adding complexity. Further, the level of complexity being added may be too insignificant. However, as complexity gets added several times over across various transactions, the entire process may become too complex for people being motivated to follow it. Let me illustrate. Let us say you have a tax mechanism whereby you collect tax from all farmers based on the size of their land holding. Let us say the farmers cultivate various varieties of crops. It could be possible that you want farmers to start cultivating certain crops which they are not cultivating today, so you may decide to give a tax reduction to farmers cultivating those crops. Farmers in a particular geographical area may request you to reduce the rate of tax applicable to them because the acreage in that geographical area is lesser compared to others. A particular village may face a natural calamity and you may decide to waive off all tax payable by farmers of that village. Now, compare a tax system which calculates tax based on a flat rate per acre of land held to a system which apart from doing this makes various concessions to the flat rate. Which system will be simpler?"

"The first one, of course. However, in case of the three examples of exceptions that you cited, the objective of each of them was absolutely correct. The situation demanded the exceptions, and hence adding complexity would have been fine in each of those cases."

"I agree – I just wanted to demonstrate how we end up adding complexity, though we want simplicity. The important part is that every time you add complexity, it should be done after a very conscious study. Complexity may mean benefits, it also means additional costs. As soon as there are exceptions to a rule, the cost of administering the rule goes up. If you have a tax system with the three exceptions I mentioned, and may be many more, it will be that much more difficult to educate people on the system and ensure compliance. You may need to add to the people strength of the tax department to administer the system. So, cost will go up. Hence, before adding complexity, a cost benefit analysis is essential to decide whether the complexity is warranted. We can also look at how the desired objective can be achieved through a simpler alternative.

"I will give you two examples of bringing in simplicity which were implemented by teams I was part of. The first one happened at the kingdom in Far East, where I had spent some time working with the new King. The second one was in the University that I offered my services to.

"The first example related to a problem of uniforms for soldiers. The military of this state had twelve different levels within, and each level had a uniform with a different colour. Further, there were four standard sizes of uniforms depending on the size of the soldier. So, in short, there were forty eight variants of uniforms that were required. With such a large number of variants, there were frequent cases of inventory goof ups, large investment in inventory, wastage, shortages of uniforms when required, etc. All of this meant on one side the costs went up, on the other, availability of required size and colour was not assured. We started working on this problem. The first thing we attempted doing is bringing down the number of levels. After a lot of discussion and debate, we brought the number of levels from twelve to seven. So, the problem was nearly halved with the number of variants going down to twenty eight. Then, another idea was generated. The objective of the colour system was easy identification of the level of the soldier from his uniform. The idea came in as we looked at what other alternative could be used to meet this objective. The idea was that instead of having a different colour uniform per level, we could divide the uniform into two sections – the base uniform, and the scarf. We could then apply the colour scheme only to the scarf while keeping the base uniform of the same colour. Once this idea got implemented, the number of variants for the base uniform went down drastically to four. In addition, there was a stock of scarfs in seven different colours that had to be maintained. The scarfs were of standard fit-all size, and hence no size variants were required. So, a problem of forty eight variants was reduced to eleven variants. The inventory of the basic uniform significantly reduced, while there was a higher stock of scarfs kept, which was a lower cost item. By doing this, the total inventory went down drastically from about two years' requirement to two months' requirement in value terms. Wastage was almost zero, and availability rose from forty eight percent to ninety three percent."

"Wow. That was brilliant."

"Standardization is one basic method of bringing in simplicity. Whether in the tax system or inventory – minimum variants or exceptions improves simplicity and simplicity improves efficiency.

"The second example, which took place in the University, relates to planning for cooking at the University canteen. The University housed thousands of students, and there was a large turnover of students coming in and traveling out almost every day. Plus, there used to be a significant number of visitors coming in. The security department of the university had a process of keeping data of people coming in and going out, which it would pass on to the canteen department, so that the canteen department could plan the number of students and others to cook for. However, the security department had number of other tasks to perform. They made mistakes regularly, and the canteen department ended up having surpluses or shortages. Number of improvements were attempted. Constant training was given to the security staff. The number of entry and exit gates was reduced from three to one for better control. This reduced the magnitude of the problem, but did not resolve it. The problem persisted. One day, a junior employee from the canteen department came up with an idea. He said, instead of relying on data coming from someone else, how if we do our own data collection? He also suggested how we could do it – by counting the number of footwear. The University campus had a no-footwear rule in its buildings. The campus had two huge buildings, one which housed the classrooms, library and offices, and the other the dormitory. At the entrance of both the buildings, there were footwear stands, where footwear had to be kept before entering those buildings. Footwear was allowed only in the garden and playground areas. So, the idea was that every day at the cut off time, a person from the canteen department would walk to the two buildings, and do a physical count of the footwear pairs. The stands were arranged systematically; hence counting would not take a lot of time. He would then do a headcount of students in the playground or the garden, where footwear was allowed. Based on this count, the canteen department would prepare food. We implemented this idea, and the result was that accuracy levels reached almost ninety nine percent, with no single day when the food went out of stock."

"Counting footwear….. How simple…." Viklav found the idea amusing.

"And very effective." Prabuddh said. "Whereas in the first example, the simplifying technique was standardization, in this case it was doing a visual check rather than a documentary one. Your Agriculture Minister has now used the same method to check wheat stock. Only difference is that we had used the method as the primary method for data collection, while he used it as a secondary method, to confirm reports received using the documentary process."

"Yes. But I always thought that a visual check may not give hundred percent accuracy."

"You are right, it does not. But the error if any stays in tolerance limits. The benefit is that you get a first-hand view of things. If a documentary report gives a number of four people or four hundred people, there is no way one can differentiate the two numbers because the numbers come from a piece of paper.

But if a visual check gives a tally of say three hundred eighty people, one knows that four hundred people could more or less be right. With the new method of counting people, we experienced much better results because we got the actual feel of how many people were in the campus as against getting the number from another department."

"Understood."

"So that was about simplicity. The next point I am going to talk about is flexibility. This mainly applies to organizations which have a high degree of process orientation. Having processes in place, and following them, is generally very good and essential for organized functioning of the organization. However, at times, some cultures overdo the process mindset, and lose focus on the real objective. They work in a very rigid manner and are not open to a deviation, even if the situation calls for it. This is incorrect. An organization needs to remain flexible to meet the need of the hour."

"Is this not the same as making exceptions that you referred to while talking about simplicity? The exceptions are also a way of flexibility, right?"

"No. What I talked about there was exceptions that make a process complex. What I am talking about now is overruling a process."

"But a process gets created through a thorough analysis of the need for it. Then, why would you overrule it? Will it not create anarchy?"

"A process is created based on historical information that we possess of how things normally work, and what kind of situations can be anticipated. It is the right way of doing things so far as the situation is one that was anticipated. But if an exceptional situation has arisen, then the process may not be appropriate to the specific situation, and hence may need to be overruled. Take for example, today's meeting of ours. I have said earlier that discipline is important for scheduling meetings. But we decided this meeting of ours at the last minute. You may have had to cancel some of your other commitments because of this. But then, the circumstances were not normal. I have to leave tomorrow due to an emergency. So, it was imperative that we had to show some flexibility.

"The important point to note is that Process is means to the end, and not an end in itself. This awareness has to be there with us constantly. At times, we imbibe the process in ourselves and forget the end. This is when flexibility is lost. Process is there for a reason. If the reason is being fulfilled, it is fine if the process is being deviated from. But to exercise this discretion, you need people with a mature head. It is important that flexibility does not affect the sanctity of Process. Flexibility is essential, but cannot be a norm. Further, if a process deviation is allowed, it is essential to reinstate the original process as soon as possible. Say for example, you have a process that tax collection from citizens happen on a particular day of every month. Let us say the tax officer goes house to house collecting tax. If in a particular house, he finds there is a member of the house who is seriously ill, and the family is stressed and in no mood to talk anything else, he may decide to skip their tax on that occasion. This is deviation. But, he will have to keep a tab on the developments in the house, so that once situation improves, he can recover the pending tax and reinstate the process he had deviated from.

"It is very difficult to write rules about applying flexibility. It significantly depends on the specifics of the particular case. The best way to imbibe flexibility in an organization is through demonstration. If you show where and why you were flexible, the team understands where they can and should be flexible. If you also show that you were disciplined to reinstate the process as soon as it was possible, the team will learn that trait too."

"I understand the importance of flexibility. Sometimes, I feel we are over-flexible. Flexibility has become a norm, and probably because of that we fail to apply flexibility even where genuinely it is required."

"Very well said. Flexibility is an important concept. It has to be given special importance, which also means that it should be sparingly applied. If there is wholesale application, on one side process will lose sanctity, and on the other, flexibility will not get its due importance, when it is really required.

"The last two traits we will talk about are humility and being analytical. Let us take up humility first. Being humble is important for the organization as well as every member of it. The behaviour should never be that of 'having arrived' or 'know-all' kind. It is necessary to be respectful to people and to their views. Every person has some unique strength. By not being humble, we do disservice to ourselves, because in that case, we do not give adequate importance to other people, their views, approaches, understanding and ideas, and thereby deprive ourselves of being benefitted from them. Strong leaders are not those who know everything, but the ones who are open to consider views and ideas of anyone. A leader works only through team work, and personal ego is the biggest enemy of team work. Humility keeps ego in check and hence plays a crucial part. Being humble primarily requires good 'listening' skills. Humble people speak less and listen more, and listen very attentively. They ask questions rather than giving answers. They are eager to learn rather than to preach."

"Prabuddh, I always thought I was a humble person. I always respect other people, and never try to emphasize that I am greater than the person I am speaking to. However, your definition of humility is much wider, and probably I get disqualified here. I like to take my decisions myself. I think I enjoy creating ideas myself rather than asking ideas of others. I get a high when I bring something new to the organization rather than seeing someone else doing it. In that sense, I am not humble."

Prabuddh nodded. "Could be," he said, "this is something for you to think about."

"Hmm... I will spend some time reflecting on this aspect."

"Good. Let me now take up the final trait, that of being analytical. Many times, people decide on matters based on their gut feel. This approach is very effective so far as speed is considered. But the problem is that the gut feel is driven by our mind, and the mind is a tricky player. It does several things which may be logically unexplainable. The mind can make us believe something that is completely non-factual; it can make us like and sometimes long for things which are actually detrimental to us. The mind works primarily based on how it has been conditioned over years. Based on the conditioning, it chooses to see only those aspects of a particular event, which it is comfortable with. Frequently, it happens that some people see only the positive side of things, and some only negative. This means, the gut feel can cheat you either ways. Hence, to arrive at the right decision, it is necessary to do analytical work. The analysis helps to give a logical basis for reinforcing or rejecting the decision which has come from the gut feel. Analysis plays another important role of getting the team convinced about the decision. A team cannot contribute to the gut feel or intuition of one person, but it can contribute to analytical work. Hence, when the decision is a gut-feel decision based on what someone 'feels', the accountability for the decision is never owned by the team, it remains with the 'someone' who made the decision. On the other hand, the analytical work can be done by the whole team; it can be viewed by the whole team. The decision taken based on the analysis becomes the team's decision, with accountability resting with the whole team.

"We experienced this when we talked about the school project. You wanted to agree to the project based on your emotional inclination. But there was no analytical work done. The analytical work done told you how the project fits into your resource budget, what changes may be required to make it successful, what other things can be incorporated keeping long term view in mind, etc. The analytical work is crucial for making the right decision and successful implementation of the decision. Hence, every action taken has to be supported with an analytical background and this has to be made an integral part of how an organization works."

Viklav was silently and very attentively listening to Prabuddh. Prabuddh sipped some water. "I am done," he said, "I have now passed to you all that I wanted to. This conceptual knowledge will guide you every day, every time. It is very important to absorb this knowledge thoroughly. The theory section of our training and my contribution to the process now stands completed. Reflecting on the theory and practical application of these concepts is a never ending job. Your part of the training will continue. Every day, every incident you face, you will have to check back on the concepts, and take actions accordingly. This is how you will get into the habit of looking at every situation from a culture perspective. The practical application will also help in giving a better understanding of the theoretical knowledge."

"Yes, Prabuddh. I will spend time in reflecting on each of these concepts. You have given me a wealth of knowledge. There is a lot of work I have to do to establish clarity in my mind on each of these concepts. My understanding of concepts has many times been far different from the perspective that you have brought in. I also find that there are certain concepts which I completely agree with, but do not always adhere to while taking actions or making decisions. I have understood that my training is not over, and it will not get over in the near future. Probably, it will not get over ever. I have to learn every day. I have to practice every day. I have to consciously work towards culture building every day. While I agree on this front, I do not agree that your contribution to the training is over. In a way, I think I am not going to miss you, because you will always remain here with me through the knowledge you have shared with me. Every time I face a problem, I am going to imagine me narrating the problem to you, and you telling me how to deal with it. Your company has influenced me a lot. I think now I will be able to guess what you would have said about any problem. So, in that sense, you will continue training me, though you will not be here physically. You always said that you have nothing new to share, it is old knowledge that you have organized better and differently. But I have learnt a whole lot of new things. If not new things, new approaches to the same things. I can feel a change within me, and I am sure my organization will have a new look and face over the next few months. Thanks to you, Prabuddh. I do not think I can thank you enough for whatever you have shared with me."

"Thanks to you too," Prabuddh said, "Thanks for your hospitality and readiness to consider new viewpoints. I have also enjoyed your company, and our discussions have been a source of learning for me too. I am sure you will now spend majority of your time in Tier zero and let culture take care of the rest of the organization. Let me wish you the best in terms of success for all your efforts. My only expectation is your commitment to the process. There will be situations that will test your resolve; you will feel like going back to your earlier style of working. But you will have to resist that temptation and always have sustainability and spontaneity as you guide."

"Prabuddh, I stand committed to this process. I promise that every action I take, every decision I make, and every word I utter will be a consciously taken step towards building culture."

"Excellent. Just a final word. I am a student of spirituality. My goal is spiritual growth for me and the society I live in. For me, spirituality means leading a blissful life. To achieve spiritual growth, we need to monitor our use of energy. Every person is driven by energy and so is the whole word. Spirituality helps us use minimum energy to achieve what we want to. If you carefully look at each culture trait that we discussed, they all lead to making the organization energy-efficient. Whether it is being 'integrated', 'learning', 'focused', 'controlled', 'disciplined', and so on… the common thread is achieving more with less. I always like to illustrate this with a comparison between a group of stray dogs and a flock of birds. The dogs run around with no purpose and no method. They are highly energy-inefficient. But a flock of birds flies in an organized way. It manages to conduct its flight with the best energy conserving methods, helping the birds to find food and protect themselves from enemies. It also appears aesthetically beautiful.

"I wish you administration becomes like a flock of birds – efficient and beautiful. While spiritual growth may not be your objective, if you achieve the management improvement that you want, you will be anyways moving on the path of spiritual growth.

Best wishes for this journey."

Viklav touched Prabuddh's feet as a mark of respect. "God bless you," Prabuddh said, as the purity of his voice and his smile spread all over the room.

Section III

The End and the Beginning

The Letter

Prabuddh was sitting under a large banyan tree. He had just finished lunch with all his disciples. The disciples had planned a group discussion on a case study that Prabuddh had presented to them. The discussion was to be done in two groups. Satatv was going to lead one of the groups. He had gone through a prolonged sickness, but had recovered well after overcoming it. Prabuddh's return from Paryaakul had helped him to stand on his feet again. Prabuddh's presence with him had given him the required strength to fight the illness and defeat it. It took a while for him to be as energized as earlier and get back to his routine. Prabuddh was a relieved man seeing him back in action as he was one of his best students.

Prabuddh was not going to join the group discussion. He had reserved this time to read a letter he had received from Viklav. The letter had come in the previous day, delivered by a messenger. Prabuddh was eager to know what was happening at Paryaakul. But the letter was quite lengthy, hence Prabuddh thought it would be best to read it later at a time when he could go through the entire letter at one go.

Prabuddh opened the letter and started reading it.

"Respected Mitr Prabuddh,

"Please accept my greetings. Hope everything is fine with you, your Ashram and your disciples. I had earlier got the news that Satatv, whose illness had forced you to travel back to your Ashram urgently, had recovered after you went back. I wish him the best of health. Your concern for one of your disciples was another lesson for me to learn. It taught me how important 'People' and 'Caring' are in building culture. I am sure Satatv will go on to become a successful practitioner of your teachings.

"It was not a surprise to me that Satatv's health improved once you were there. The health of my organization has seen a similar effect since you have been here. It has been almost three months since you returned back, but there was not even one day in this period that I did not think about you, about culture, and about the concepts you shared with me. Culture has now become like my breath, it is there with me wherever and whatever I am doing. I consciously think about culture all the time. The important thing is that I am seeing a similar transformation in the organization, in every person. They are also practicing culture the way I want them to, knowingly or unknowingly. The difference is that I have formally learnt the conceptual background of what I am doing, they have not. They are practicing culture because they have seen me doing it, and they have seen me talking about it. I have also experienced that they are passing the culture trail to the next level the way I did to them. It is all happening at a slow pace, but it is taking a definite and firm route reaching to the last point in the organization. I can see your thoughts that you sowed in my mind spread and blossom across the organization. At this point I realize that if I can consciously modify the way that the organization behaves, the culture that got developed over years was also on my account. Earlier, it got developed without me realizing it, and now

I am making a conscious effort to implement the new culture. Earlier, whenever I would come across a non-satisfactory behaviour of any member of the organization, I would try to find fault with the person. Now, I realize that in each of these situations, I was equally responsible, because the behaviour is an expression of the culture, and the source of culture in the organization is me. I create culture, either through action or through inaction. The first time you mentioned to me that culture is my baby, I was in a state of shock. Today, that concept appears obvious to me. I will remain indebted to you for bringing this realization to me; for telling me that the problem is me, and so is the solution.

"You shared with me several other concepts – how to create culture, what are the important constituent traits of good culture, what each of the constituent actually means, etc. These concepts were not completely new to me, but their presentation was. Today, just like the concept of culture being driven by the leader, these concepts also appear very obvious to me. But, the odd fact is that I never really paid attention to these concepts earlier. They were never important enough to me. I was always busy waging wars, building roads, dams and bridges, solving problems on hand, making decisions and instructing people. My organization did what I told them to do. But two major pillars of success – sustainability and self-sufficiency were missing. Things were fine till I acted. If I did not or could not, things just stopped. Nothing would happen automatically, or on its own. Nothing would continue on its own. Probably, in a way, I got used to it. Probably, I enjoyed it. But you brought in the awareness in me that this was wrong. I realized that the organization has to work in a sustainable and spontaneous way – with or without me. I realized that the only way to ensure that the organization works when I am not around, is by ensuring that it works when I am around without my intervention. I continued to intervene, but in a different way. Earlier, I made my people to act. Now, I make them think. The thought in turn makes them act. Once a person does a particular activity over number of times, he develops the habit of doing that activity. My people were earlier habituated to acting, after I had instructed them to act. Now, they are developing the habit of thinking, and their thinking is making them act. I have practiced this over last few months – with huge success. In a way, you followed the same principle while working on me. I was looking for a solution outside. You told me to find it within. I have done the same to my team. This is moving like a chain reaction.

"We are a different organization today, far different from what we were before you came in. I know there is scope for further improvement. This is just the beginning. But I am very happy and I want to thank you immensely for showing me the right path and teaching me how to walk on it. Your method of teaching which does not give the solution but teaches how to get the solution in itself is a 'spontaneous' and a 'sustainable' method. I have been lucky to have your company and guidance which has been great for my organization for sure, but has also made an immense impact on me and my perspective of life, in general.

"Thanks a lot, Prabuddh. I wish you all the very best in your endeavor of working on organizational culture as a means to reach spiritual progress of the society. At any stage in your work, if you think I can play a role, I will be more than happy to help.

"At this point, I want to share with you some of the developments that have occurred at our end. During your stay at Paryaakul, we had discussed of various initiatives/ transactions that we were looking at. There is progress on each of these initiatives. Some new developments have also come up during this period. I have annexed to this letter a gist of all that has taken place since you left. This will give you an indication of how we have progressed.

"I have separately annexed a summary of the key points that you discussed with me. I use this summary as a guide to refer to whenever I am unsure. I also go through the summary on a regular basis. I had promised you that I would give you a copy of the summary, hence I am sending it with this letter.

Hoping I get an opportunity to meet you in person soon,

Culturally yours,

Viklav"

Prabuddh closed the letter and sat silently for a few minutes reflecting on the message. He felt happy with the contents. He then moved to the annexures.

Update

“A nnexure I – Updates from the Paryaakul kingdom

1. Wheat inventory management

I had to put this update at the number one position because this was one matter we discussed almost at every meeting between you and me. The processes that we put in place with respect to this area are working very well. I am getting a monthly report on both, the actual inventory of wheat, and the status of processes followed during that month. While the inventory report gives the actual quantity of wheat in stock, I give more importance to the process report. The process report tells me how the weekly reports were made, who checked them, when the physical visit was done by the Minister, etc. Several suggestions have been coming from the team members about improvements or additions to the processes put in place. One such suggestion was that the existing stock be divided into two halves, stored at two different locations. All stock issues to happen only from one location. Once the stock at the first location is completely exhausted, only then the second location to be brought in use. This, to also be used as a trigger to start the ordering process for the next consignment as an inter-lock. I liked this idea a lot. However, the entire responsibility for considering such ideas and deciding on them is with the Agriculture Minister. He has to decide and come to me only for informing or consulting, not for decision making. I will be doing regular follow up with him on this particular idea. I am confident we will not have a failure on this issue, ever again.

2. Office start time

The new policy as regards the strict implementation of office start time has worked well. The delay allowed has now been brought down to only five minutes. But what we have actually seen is that almost everybody comes in well before the start time, rather than during the five minute delay period. It has been a brilliant display of how team work works, and of how old habits can be changed. While this success story continues, the People Minister has recently approached me with an issue – that of people being in the offices beyond their work time. He made a report that almost fifty percent of the time, our people work extra hours. This, it appears, has been a practice for several years. I am really happy that the People Minister has now realized that this practice is incorrect. Probably, the cultural change in him has made him think in this manner. Nonetheless, I have told him that this is a serious issue and needs to be dealt with appropriately. So many people working extra time is not fair, it is also an indicator of inefficiency or shortage of people. I have asked the Minister to take up this matter with the Council, and the matter to be managed like any other project in a similar way like how the start time issue was looked at.

3. Communication platforms

I have given special importance to the structure part of culture, the P-P-C. One biggest achievement over the last three months has been establishing and successful operation of communication platforms. It started with the meetings of the Council of Ministers without me. Once this clicked, it has now become the new norm of communication. Earlier, there was no quality communication between the Ministers till I came in. Within their departments, the Ministers were practicing a similar method. Their teams would wait for the Minister to initiate intra-team communication. Within three months, the situation has completely reversed. Now, we see free flow of communication between people, without waiting for a catalyst! The improvement in communication has helped team spirit to grow. It has also ensured that problems get discussed at the team level before they are escalated. Many of them get resolved at that stage itself, so a lesser number of problems come to the top. I have started finding a lot of free time more recently because of this. I see the same happening with my Ministers. This was not an easy journey though. I had to put in consistent effort in creating this habit. People had got used to a particular way of working – they liked to come to me with every problem. They were not comfortable taking up issues with peer teams on their own. They were also not comfortable making decisions without my intervention. But every time they came to me, I resisted my natural response, and I sent them back to follow the new method of working. Over time, they did accept the new method. But interestingly, probably without them knowing about it, they have implemented the same methods in their respective departments. I think we have done a splendid job in this area. As an effect of this, we are now seeing a large number of suggestions coming from down. Teams are thinking on problems, and coming up with ways of dealing with them, proactively. I can actually feel pressure of action coming to me from my subordinates, and they are feeling a similar pressure from their juniors. The direction of pressure has suddenly changed, and I am enjoying this pressure. It is my duty, and that of every leader in the administration to encourage the suggestions, the pressure, and to reciprocate at the same speed with an action, or a decision – an acceptance or a rejection, with of course the reasoning behind it. I think we are doing this well.

4. The Finance Minister

The Finance Minister's behaviour has shown slow, but good progress. He has been participating well in the Council meetings. His communication may still not be very proactive with the team, but I ensure that there are ample opportunities for him to interact with every team member, rather than only me. Whenever he comes to me with information that should have been first shared with a team member, I politely send him back. Whenever he comes to me with a question he should rather have asked of a team member, I do the same. I can understand that behaviour patterns of a resource as senior as him cannot change in a day. But the good part is that there is some improvement, and for a change, I see him smiling more often in our group meetings.

5. Process register & Incident register

On the Process front, I have initiated a project to document all processes that we follow in the organization. I have noticed that frequently, a process that is initiated remains in practice till the person who initiated it is in charge. If another person comes in his place, the process may get lost. Similarly, we may have an excellent process in a specific area in a specific department. But similar areas in other departments that may benefit from this process are not even aware about it. Taking this into consideration, I want to create an exhaustive document listing and detailing the processes across the organization. Just like other projects, I have handed this project to the team. They have liked it and have taken up the project in the right spirit. In fact, the team came up with the idea of doing regular process audits to ensure that the processes documented have been properly followed. Another similar project taken up is what I call an 'Incident register'. Any event in the organization which needs special attention will get recorded in the Incident register. It could be a failure, a deficiency identified, etc. Every incident will be analysed by the team. They will study it in depth, and try to reach the root cause of the problem, and derive a process solution to it. This solution will get implemented – it will follow the 'culture creation' process. This process will then get added to the Process register. Both these projects are only at an introduction stage. The Incident register has been initiated with a few entries already done. The process register should take about a month to be completed.

6. Process for new projects

We have finalized the process to deal with new projects at proposal stage. With respect to every project proposal, it will first pass through a synopsis stage. At this stage, all important points with respect to the Project will be captured, but with lesser accuracy and not in depth. The objective is dual. The first objective is to get a first level check on the project before undertaking a detailed study. The second objective is to get the whole team involved in the subject much before the detailed project study is undertaken. This helps in getting the team prepared, so that the next stages can take place quickly. With respect to the synopsis as well as the detailed report, standard formats have been prepared. All projects will get taken up at the Council meetings before creating recommendations for me.

7. Meetings

I have had a complete relook at how meetings are scheduled. To ensure meetings start in time, I now schedule my meetings with a cushion of ten minutes between two meetings. The on-time performance of my meetings has improved because of this. My assistant does an analytical report to me every day on the performance. If there is any material failure on this part, I conduct a root cause analysis along with the assistant and correct the scheduling process accordingly.

I am also very serious about the conduct of meetings. I ensure that meetings are scheduled in advance, so teams can be prepared for them. But during the meeting, no diversions are allowed to the pre decided agenda. I sent back meeting teams on two occasions for not being prepared. This strong message has helped in improving the conduct of meetings significantly thereafter.

8. Checklists

Checklists have now become a part of our routine. I refer to my checklist every day without fail. My assistant helps me in managing my checklist. This tool has helped me immensely in managing affairs and exercising 'control'. I have become very particular with how the Council members manage their affairs. I have introduced the concept of checklist to each one of them, and all of them have adopted this tool, some quickly, others after a lot of follow up. They have now seen how useful this tool is, and now it is becoming a habit for them. I have also been informed that they have taken this tool to the next level team, and I am sure that in some more time, the checklist will be used by every person in our organization. My day begins with the checklist, since it helps me prioritize, plan, and structure my day better, and makes me disciplined as regards use of my time.

9. People profile

The creation of platforms for communication has helped in improving the 'C' part. The process register and the Incident register are aimed at improving the second 'P'. Now, let me write about what we have done with respect to the first 'P' – People. I have initiated another project in this area, which has moved well and swiftly. The People department is playing a major role here. We have undertaken to profile every person in the organization. We want to create a master file recording every person's strengths, weaknesses, potential, history, etc. This is being done through discussions with everyone concerned - the person himself, his superior, his peers and his team. At the end of this project, we want to reach a stage wherein we should completely know every person in the administration and have a plan for growth of every person. This document will be reviewed fully once a year and revised based on new knowledge gained. There will be a process for one-to-one meetings between every person and his superior on a quarterly basis to identify and deal with any issues coming up between the annual reviews. The People profile will play a major role in keeping the motivation level of people high. On the macro side, it will indicate skill set availability to the organization, deficiencies in specific skill sets, etc. On the micro side, there will be a plan for every person, areas needing attention will come out proactively, and issues will get dealt with as close as possible to their emergence.

10. The school project

The school project has had significant developments. The Education Minister submitted a detailed proposal in this regard a few weeks after you went back. The team decided to go ahead with the secondary school and Agriculture specialization. The piece of land has been identified. Finance budgets have been worked out in detail. The plan to identify and educate graduates who wish to become teachers has been worked out. Accordingly, I have approved the project, and phase I construction has already commenced. My wife's nephew has been transferred as the

Project Manager at site, and his performance has been excellent so far. The Council gets a report from him once a week, and the entire project gets discussed on a weekly basis. I do a review with the Council, but it is a quick one, and usually only to get information. Only once during the last three months, the Council required my intervention, when some locals raised a concern that the land chosen for the school complex was being used as a grazing land for their cattle, and were worried that their dairy production may get affected. We got into an arrangement with them to allow them to continue using a part of the land currently being used by them for their cattle. In return, they would supply milk to the school hostel at a pre-determined price for the first five years. They would also give cow dung and cow urine free of cost, which would help creating pesticides and manure for the Agriculture specialization wing. To accommodate the farmers, the building plan had to be revised, since the building location had to be shifted westwards, where construction cost was higher due to uneven land. Though there was additional upfront cost, it worked alright on a return on investment basis. Slight changes to the phase wise schedule were done, so that the extra expense could be taken up in the second year, since year one budget was fully used up. The project is progressing well, and remains on target, on time and cost parameters for now, after considering the revised costs.

I have also received a report from the Education Minister on the new proposed policy for decentralizing of higher education. I have only gone through it and need to study in detail before approving. But the brief reading that I did tells me that the report has been done after a thorough study, and will be good to implement.

The Foreign Affairs Minister has taken up writing to his counterparts in the neighboring kingdoms introducing them to the proposal for the Agriculture education being made available to their citizens at a cost. The proposal has received positive response. We will be working out the details in course of time.

11. Suggestions

A very positive development observed over the last thirty to forty five days has been a surge in the number of suggestions coming from our colleagues. There have been suggestions of all kinds pouring in. Some are excellent, some inferior. But the important point is that the people are thinking – thinking for the organization. They are also freely communicating their ideas, and senior teams are entertaining those ideas. That is how so many suggestions are reaching right up to me. Taking cognizance of this, the People Minister has created a process around managing suggestions. A suggestion register has been created. Every suggestion gets analyzed by a team made out of members of the Council, and gets allotted to a particular Minister. The suggestion gets taken to its logical conclusion, which is then communicated back to the person who generated the solution. Suggestions which are really good are rewarded with a cash award. This may have been put in place for slightly more than a month, but it has been working so well, it appears as if we have been doing this for ages. Some of the suggestions look at things so very differently; I am now fully convinced on how diverse approaches from team members can add value. I also now understand that people at all levels have intelligence, but they use it and come forward to share it, only if there is an encouraging environment around them. I am going to share two such suggestions that caught my eye with you. These suggestions are still in the process of being studied. However, I was amazed seeing them, as to how differently people can think. These suggestions appear as obvious alternatives today, but no one ever thought about them earlier.

The first suggestion has come from a manager in the People department. We have created a system of messengers for quick communication of urgent matters. We are a large kingdom, and if any urgent information has to be passed from one point to another, we use the service of these messengers. Their service is meant for use by the administration, but at times, the trading community and certain individuals also use their service if any urgent message is to be passed on to business connects or to family. The messengers are horse-riders who are kept in an 'always ready' position, so that they can move at any time usually carrying a written message from one administrative team to another. Most of the times, their movement is from the regional headquarters to the capital city. The messengers, on certain days, would travel long distances at short notice, and then for several days, they would have no work. Both of these affect their health. There have been instances where the messengers have fallen ill, and there was a case where a messenger died during travel due to exhaustion. Currently, we have messengers at twenty nine locations. The idea suggested changing the system of point-to-point communication to a hub and spoke system with relay transmission of messages. The manager suggests creating seven hubs and allotting spokes to each hub based on geographical proximity. Irrespective of whether there is a message to be transmitted or not, a messenger will make a regular trip to the hub, so that incoming messages could be collected. So, every message will pass through three communication segments – spoke to hub, hub to hub and hub to spoke. As per the manager, the advantage of this system will be uniform distribution of work. Each messenger will have more regular work, but will not have to travel large distances at one go. As per the estimates presented by him, the average distance traveled per day by each messenger will go up, however the wide variation in distance traveled on a daily basis will come down sharply. While the system will keep messengers occupied every day, there will not be any overload on them on a specific day. There will be some delay in transmission of messages to the destination as compared to the earlier system, but it needs to be studied as to what magnitude it will be and whether we can live with it.

The second suggestion has come from quite a junior position in the Agriculture department. This is a mind-boggling one. Our kingdom is currently made of four states. All the states are vertically stacked one above the other. Each of the state has a coast line to the west, mountain range at the centre, and plains to the right. The east border of all states is more or less aligned, except the northern most state, which has a large section of plains much further to the east as compared to the other three states. The organization of states in this manner was merely by chance. We have maintained the structure of the states that we took over from other kingdoms. Our departments are structured in a way that every department has teams dedicated to individual states, apart from the general administration team. The idea this person has suggested is to change the structure of the states from what it is currently to a topography-based structure. He suggests that we create a coastal state covering all sea-level area, a mountain state covering the mountain range, and a plateau state covering the plains. His reasoning behind this is that certain topography suits certain type of activity. Specific crops grow in specific areas, the fertility of soil differs, labour productivity also differs. The kind of non-farming occupations practiced are different – the coastal belt has predominantly fishing activity, the mountains have forest-based occupations like honey gathering, the plains have a lot of dairy and livestock rearing. The food habits, the weather patterns, the living styles, are also vastly different in these three geographical belts. Of the four states, headquarters of three are in the coastal belt. The fourth state's headquarters are in the plains. Development, somehow, gets concentrated where the headquarters lie, and other geographic belts do not get their due share of attention and fund allocation. This creates imbalanced growth of districts within the kingdom. An important point raised by him is about costs. Every departmental state team has to incur additional costs as each of them has to manage all three geographic belts within it. The cost of travel itself is substantial as moving from one belt to another is not easy. Further, the state teams have to create organizational strength to manage all three belts. For example, all four state teams have to invest effort in development of fishing activity in the coast, honey gathering and Ayurveda medicines in the mountains, and dairy, meat and agriculture in the plains. It also makes them less efficient as there is lesser specialization. The state specific teams have members coming from a specific geographic background, who may not fully understand the requirements or difficulties of other geographical areas. For example, the mountain region which is the least populated, covering about ten percent of the entire population, never gets adequate representation in the state teams of any state of any department of the administration, and hence, the administration loses out on the on-ground knowledge of issues of that region.

This is a ground breaking suggestion. I fell in love with it as soon it came before me. I am just delighted with the approach of the person who came up with the suggestion, and I keep asking why none of us ever thought about it earlier. I am sure this idea would have come to this person much earlier. Possibly, he did not care to share it because he may have thought that sharing may not be of much use. The changed environment made him put forth the suggestion, and how brilliant it is! I am really excited about it. If I was my earlier version, I would have already started acting on it. But, I also have changed. While I am fascinated by the idea of the reorganization, I want a thorough study made on it before any action is taken. I understand that if we have to pursue this idea, it may be a multi- year project. There will be costs involved in creating or reorganizing the infrastructure and the reporting structure. It will take a huge effort to do what we want to do. Hence, the idea has been given back to the Council to look at it in depth and report their initial findings on benefits, concerns, costs, etc. We will have to estimate what kind of monetary benefits the proposal can deliver in the medium to long term, and whether that can offset the upfront costs required. We will need to validate the efficiency improvement that we believe will be experienced. Ultimately, the welfare of citizens has to improve with this project, if it has to be implemented. It is going to be a mammoth project, and I want to lead it, of course, with complete team involvement, and in a very professional manner.

I am very happy with these suggestions and others coming in from the team, which indicates a fundamental feeling of belonging that the people have developed to the organization. I can see our march towards becoming a truly self-sufficient and sustainable organization.

Prabuddh, I am feeling nice after having written on all the above updates. I was very eager to share with you all these developments at our end. Speaking to you was always an enriching and calming experience, but having written this letter has also given me a similar feeling, as if you were here with me. I and my kingdom were really lucky, to have you with us, and I hope there will be more opportunities for us to interact in the future."

Summary

A nnexure II – Summary

Objective of culture

To make an organization:

- Sustainable, and
- Self-sufficient

Culture synopsis

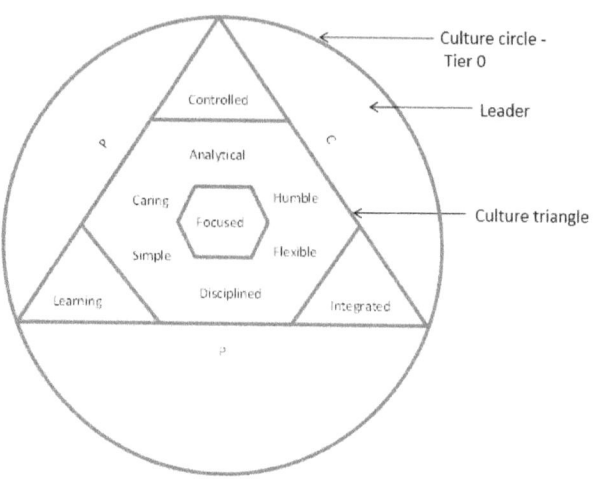

Culture circle - Tier 0

Leader

Culture triangle

Culture creation process

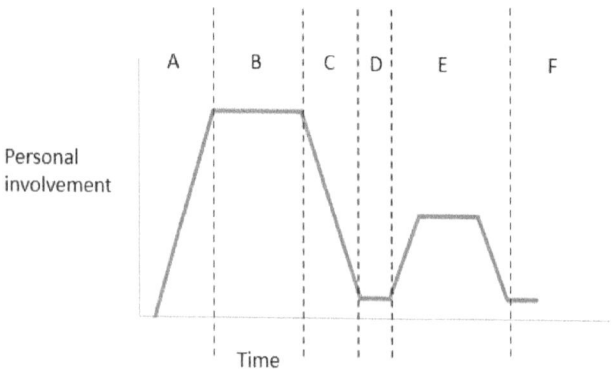

Dimensions of culture

- People
- Process
- Communication

The three dimensions are perspectives to look at everything that happens in an organization. Balanced growth of all three is essential for developing the right culture. Every culture transaction is a C-P-P-C loop. For understanding and changing culture, a culture transaction needs to be analysed at the level of individual C-P-P-C loops and the lowest unit of P-P-C in play.

Basic concepts of culture

Culture is:

- the 'way of life' of a group of people
- automatic; it happens by itself
- continuous, practiced every day
- always top-driven
- dynamic, can change over time in any direction
- programmable

Culture is what is demonstrated

- The leader defines, implements and demonstrates culture. Demonstration is the most important part of culture building.
- If demonstrated culture is different from the defined one, the demonstrated culture always wins.
- Demonstration of culture contrary to the defined one can take place in two ways – active and passive.
- Active demonstration takes place when the leader himself acts contrary to the defined culture.
- Passive demonstration takes place when the leader takes no action in spite of being aware of behaviour by a team member which is contrary to the defined culture.

Culture is what the 'top' does

- The senior team in an organization has a significant influence on culture.
- It is more important for the leader to correct culture at the top rather than at the lower levels.
- Damage done to the defined culture is much higher when a senior member acts contrary to the defined culture.

Culture Snippets

Culture:

- Is at 'Tier zero'.
- Is a 'core support' function
- Is the most important function for an organization, on a long-term basis
- Can never be delegated
- Is not linked to genetics
- Cannot be created by talking or writing it; but only reinforced through it

Leadership Snippets

- True leadership is constantly challenging people to grow
- Involve people, do not instruct them
- No one is bigger than the purpose, not even the leader
- Leadership means leading from behind, and coming to the front only when the situation demands

Constituents of right culture

'Centre group'

- Focused

'Corner group'

- Integrated
- Learning
- Controlled

'Mid-centre group'

- Caring
- Simple
- Flexible
- Disciplined
- Humble
- Analytical

Focused: _DOING MORE OF LESS_

- Every transaction, decision, action should be in line with the Focus
- There has to be adequate resource for every project undertaken, else projects which individually are in line with the Focus, may actually turn against it
- Maintaining tempo of an initiative is important
- Multi-tasking is counter-productive if it means doing several things at the same time

---

Integrated: _REINFORCEMENT THAT STRENGTHENS_

- Free flowing, quality communication is a must
- Strong bonds required amongst team members
- Need proper platforms for communication flow

Learning: *MISTAKES ARE GOOD, PROVIDED WE LEARN FROM THEM*

- The root cause of every mistake needs to be identified
- A solution needs to be created for the 'cause'
- The solution has to be communicated and internalized
- Repetitions of failures should be separately tracked and dealt with
- The 'Learning' process should be made 'visual' through records of mistakes and solutions

Controlled: *PLAN NING SHOULD BE END TO END*

- Detailed planning required with sequential steps of activities
- The plan of activities needs to be converted to a checklist with a plan for review by line item
- The plan should identify critical areas and provide for stringent reviews thereof
- It should also provide for alternative plans in critical areas
- Review to be conducted at pre-defined schedule of the listed items
- Action to be initiated based on outcome of the review

Caring: *PEOPLE ARE ASSETS; 'MAINTAIN' THEM*

- Caring for people primarily means caring for their 'minds'
- People need to be given opportunity to work in teams
- People need to be made felt important; they need to be told how important their work is; their opinions need to be 'listened' to
- People need to be given a clearly defined role and reporting structure
- People's work needs to be reviewed; good work appreciated and mistakes pointed out to help them improve
- People need to be challenged with new roles and new problems

Simple: *ACHIEVING SIMPLICITY IS NOT SIMPLE*

- Complexity adds cost. Before adding the smallest bit of complexity, a cost-benefit analysis should be done
- Simple processes are always easy to implement
- Two important tools for achieving simplicity are 'standardization' and making things 'visual'.

Flexible: *PROCESS IS IMPORTANT, BUT NOT AS MUCH AS THE OBJECTIVE*

- People need to have maturity to override process when there is a genuine need
- Process is means to end, not an end in itself
- Process can be deviated temporarily, but it is the duty of the person deviating to reinstate it as soon as possible
- Flexibility can only be sparingly applied

Disciplined: *DISCIPLINE SHOULD BE EXERCISED WITH A LOT OF DISCIPLINE*

- Discipline is about using resources with care
- The scarcest resource is time. Time should always be valued, that of every person
- Scheduling meetings and conduct thereof has to be done with utmost care

Humble: *RESPECT EVERYBODY*

- It is important to be open to ideas from anybody
- People need to be given importance; attentive listening to what they say is key
- Personal egos need to be kept out

Analytical: *ANALYSE BEFORE DECIDING*

- What people 'feel' can mislead them into making incorrect decisions
- Analysis provides a logical foundation to a decision
- 'Feel' is personal; Analysis can be done in teams or can be demonstrated to teams - decisions based on analysis help in driving the entire team's focus and effort towards the decision

About the author

Ashish Marathe is a chartered accountant with 15 years of experience in the corporate world. He has primarily worked in areas of Finance and Strategy. As a part of his Strategy experience, he learnt that while 'what' things to do is the core focus an organization needs, it has to give equal importance to 'how' to do those things. The internal strengthening of an organization helps it to deal with the external circumstances better. This is the philosophy Ashish believes in, which he has propagated through this book. He believes culture plays a huge role in building the internal strength; hence he has focused on summarizing the 'science' of culture through this book.

Ashish stays in Goa, India, with his parents, wife and a 5 year old son.